HISTORIC WEST WALES

Paul R. Davis

CHRISTOPHER DAVIES

Copyright © Paul R. Davis 1992.

Published by
Christopher Davies (Publishers) Ltd.,
P.O. Box 403, Sketty, Swansea, SA2 9BE.

ISBN 0 7154 0722 8

*Printed in Wales by
Dinefwr Press, Rawlings Road, Llandybïe, Dyfed.*

Contents

INTRODUCTION

West Wales is a land of contrast: lush rolling hills of the Tywi and Teifi valleys, bleak moorlands and gorse-speckled slopes of stone-crowned mountains, and rugged cliffs under ceaseless assault by the tides. Man has lived in this changing environment for at least 12,000 years, and the relics left by the ancestors of today's inhabitants are as varied as the landscape itself.

The ancient monuments included in this book represent the dwellings, fortresses, religious shrines and burial sites of the last dozen millenia or so. Before arriving at a gazeteer section of some of the numerous monuments of west Wales, it is first necessary to outline the development of Man, so that these relics can be placed in their proper historical perspective.

For the purposes of this book, we need travel back no further than the *Upper Paleolithic*, the 'Old Stone Age', a vast period of time which lasted from about 50,000 to 10,000 BC. During this Age, northern Europe was periodically covered by extensions of the great Polar ice cap. There were, however, several interglacial periods of milder weather which broke the harsh grip of the ice, and proved more hospitable to early Man. The lonely tribes which roamed the land hunted animals such as mammoth, woolly rhinocerous, reindeer and bear with primitive stone weapons, and huddled together for warmth and shelter in the mouths of limestone caves, safe from the prowling beasts of the night. All that we have to indicate the presence of these people are their chipped flint tools, discovered by modern archaeologists, and the caves themselves, such as **Hoyle's Mouth (92)** and **Cathole (101)**, which once looked out onto a landscape vastly different from today's.

With the gradual retreat of the ice around 10,000 BC, more bands of nomadic hunters travelled across the re-shaped countryside, searching the young forests for game. With the passing of a few centuries, the glacier-scoured valleys and plains were clothed in dense forests of birch and pine, later giving way to oak, elm and alder. The rising temperature brought a rise in sea level, and around 6500 BC Britain was finally separated by the English Channel from the north European land mass. Relics of the great inundations which took place can be seen along the south and west coasts of

Hoyle's Mouth cave.

Wales; blackened, peat-like stumps and roots of submerged forests poke up through the sand at Marros, Amroth and Newgale. The period from around 10,000 to 4500 BC is known to modern historians as the *Mesolithic*, or Middle Stone Age. Weapons and tools were still made from flint or stone, painstakingly shaped by hand, but now with greater refinement. Traces of numerous flint working 'factories' have been discovered along the Welsh coast, one of the most important being at **Nab Head (126)**, where thousands of flint implements and waste from their manufacture have been uncovered.

Neolithic Age

It is to the Neolithic, or New Stone Age, that the earliest surviving above-ground monuments belong. From about 4500 BC a succession of colonists from Europe introduced a basic system of agriculture, and began clearing areas of woodland for crop planting. For the next 4000 years, monuments constructed for religious and sepulch-

Neolithic chambered tomb at Pentre Ifan.

ral rites were to dominate the landscape. The reverence and beliefs associated with death and the after-life led the early farmers to construct vast tombs to hold the bones of their dead. In Wales, where stone is abundant, these tombs were constructed of huge boulders — *megaliths* — in the form of a slab-lined *burial chamber* roofed over with a massive *capstone*. This chamber would then be surrounded by a mound either of smaller stones, a *cairn*, or of earth, a *barrow*. The cairn usually took the form of an elongated, wedge-shaped mound with the chamber at the widest end, such as **Twlc y Filiast (10)**, **Pentre-ifan (62)** and **Carn Turne (85)**. Some tombs, such as **Morfa Bychan (40)**, **Carreg Samson (141)** and **Coetan Arthur (150)** were surrounded by a circular mound. None of these monuments survives in their original form. Grave-robbers and stone-robbers have contributed to the wind and weather in despoiling the tombs, so

that today only the gaunt stone chambers remain. These isolated chambers have been known by the Welsh or Cornish names of *cromlech, dolmen* and *quoit*.

The Bronze Age

The gradual introduction of copper and bronze around 2500 BC, along with the infiltration of new concepts and beliefs, initiated a change in society, one that is highlighted by the new burial practices. The huge communal Neolithic tombs were replaced by smaller *round cairns*, with a single cremation deposit placed within a stone-lined *cist*, or coffin, and then covered over with a cairn or barrow mound. Cairns and barrows can be found in a great variety of size and shape; ring, round, platform and circle are self-descriptive cairn, types. They can also be found singly, or in groups, eg. at **Mynydd Llangyndeirn (6)**, **Foel Drygarn**

(77) and **Dry Burrows (100)**. Excavations have revealed that some Bronze Age mounds have complex internal stone settings, such as the **Llanboidy barrows (30)** and **Kilpaison (105)**, while others have prominent external features such as kerbstones; **Mynydd Llangyndeirn (6)**, and the **Dyffryn cairn circle (82)** are noteable examples.

More striking are the ceremonial monuments of this Age, the *standing stones* and *stone circles*. Although countless theories have been advanced to explain the function of these particular megalithic monuments — gravestones, sighting points, astronomical markers, fertility idols — they remain enigmatic survivors of the Prehistoric landscape. More legends are connected with these monuments than any other. Despite the writings of 18th and 19th-century antiquarians, these stones have nothing to do with the priesthood of the Druids, which flourished at the time of the Roman invasion; nor have they any connection with King Arthur, as many place-names would have us believe.

The Iron Age

From about 600 BC a succession of continental immigrants introduced a new metal to Britain, heralding the Iron Age. *Hillforts* and *defended settlements* proliferated in this period, in contrast to the mainly sepulchral and ritual monuments of the previous historic Ages. This sociological change may have been brought about by the developing Bronze Age hierarchial systems. The forts vary greatly in size and strength, from simple *univallate* enclosures with a single defensive bank and ditch, to large and complex *multivallate* sites with a series of ramparts and outer defensive works. These defences comprised a rampart (of earth or stones) topped with a timber palisade, and an outer ditch.

Bronze Age standing stone near St. David's.

Bedd Morus standing stone.

Castell Henllys; a reconstructed Iron Age round hut.

The gate was often a simple gap through the bank closed by gates and guarded by a wooden tower; but at many larger forts the entrance was protected by additional defences, such as inturned walls, a chevaux-de-frise, or a barbican annexe (see sites **17, 60, 77, 87** and **142**). Within the enclosures stood round huts with peaked thatched roofs, and other ancillary buildings such as storerooms and animal pens. Some Iron Age settlements were established on cliff-tops or promontory sites, where artifical defence was needed only on the vulnerable landward side. A great number of these promontory forts can be reached from the Pembrokeshire Coast Path, and include the impressive multi-vallate sites of **Fishponds** and **Greenala Camps (112)** and **Caerau (142)**.

All these defended enclosures varied not only in size and extent, but also in function; some of the very large sites, including **Merlin's Hill (17), Foel Drygarn (77)** and **Carn Ingli (67)** were probably used as fortified towns, or tribal refuges, while the smaller enclosures such as **Llangynog (12), Robeston Wathen (51), Henry's Moat (82)** and the **Treffgarne sites (134)** were probably farmsteads fortified for individual security. On **St David's Head (150), Stackpole Warren (112)**

Reconstruction of a typical Iron Age promontory fort.

10

and **Carn Ingli Common (67)** are traces of the agricultural activities of the Prehistoric farmers — field walls, boundaries and stock pens. Defence was not uppermost on everyone's mind, as 'open' settlements on the Preseli Mountains and at Treffgarne reveal.

The Roman Period

In the third quarter of the 1st century AD the Roman presence began to make itself felt in parts of the country. A fort was established at **Carmarthen (16)** around 80 AD, which later developed into the regional capital of the *Demetae*, the ruling Celtic tribe of this area of Wales. Despite the claims of some antiquarians and early historians, there is no certain evidence that the Romans extended their military network west of Carmarthen. It was the policy to foster the Roman way of life in a conquered territory, and it would seem that the *Demetae*, on the whole, opted for a non-aggressive stance against the invaders. The large number of Roman finds (pots, coins, imported ware, jewellery), and the existence of several 'Romanized' native farmsteads (**38, 41 and 84**), indicate that aspects of the foreign lifestyle and economy had spread to the native tribes of west Wales.

The Dark Ages

How long the *Romano-British* social structures survived the collapse of Roman power is uncertain. By the 5th century AD (the beginning of the 'Dark Ages', Irish raiders had probably settled in parts of Wales fronting the western sea. This period witnessed the growth of the *Early Christian Church*, the Word of God brought by itinerant saints and holy men. Relics of this period are restricted mainly to carved and inscribed memorial stones, the vast majority located in later churches built on the site of Early Christian burial grounds.

During the 5th and 6th centuries, stones were generally inscribed with a Latin tag such as BARRIVEND FILI VENDUBAR HIC IACIT ('Barrivendus, son of Vendubarus, he lies here'). The person commemorated would probably have been an important member of the local community, or one of the ruling classes. Some of the inscriptions were duplicated in Irish *Ogham* script, for the benefit of those settlers unfamiliar with the old Roman language. Ogham consists of a series of notches along the edge of a stone, and examples can

Detail of the carvings on the Carew cross.

be seen at **Llandawke (36), Eglwys Cymmyn (39), St Dogmael's (28)** and **Nevern (61)**. From the 7th century onwards the bilingual inscribed slabs gave way to headstones carved with a cross. These cross-stones eventually developed into masterpieces of native art, with intricate patterns, such as the great crosses of **Nevern (61)** and **Carew (99)**.

From the centres of religious learning founded by the Dark Age holy men — Dewi, Teilo, Brynach and Illtyd among them — Christianity spread through the land. Itinerant saints established small sacred precincts — *llannau* — the forerunners of the later Medieval church, and which today can be identified by place-names, surviving Dark Age stones, and circular churchyards. Such indications of antiquity can be seen at **Llangan (32), Eglwys Cymmyn (39), Bayvil (59)** and **Llandeilo (80)**.

Reconstruction of a Dark Age Llan.

The Middle Ages

During the Early Middle Ages the country was divided into numerous petty kingdoms ruled by individual kings and princes, almost ceaselessly at war with each other. A charismatic and ruthless figure might occasionally enforce some order on this turbulent situation, but with short-lived results. The rape and pillage antics of the Vikings did not help matters either. Into this unsettled land the Normans rode at the end of the 11th century. Following the conquest of lowland England in 1066, these ruthless, efficient warlords, themselves of Viking descent, pressed on into Wales, establishing frontier castles as they went, to tighten and then stabilize their grip on a conquered territory. The Normans made an occasional raid into west Wales, but with the death of Rhys ap Tewdwr, the last king of the western territory of *Deheubarth*, the way was open for a full-scale invasion. In 1093 several groups of Norman entrepreneurs marched overland, or sailed up the broad rivers, to establish castles and carve out chunks of Welsh territory for their own. In the next 200 years their claims were hotly contested by the native rulers, but with comparatively little effect.

The Norman grip on south Pembrokeshire, in particular, was so effective that a distinct cultural and linguistic division sprang up, evidenced today by the proliferation of English sounding place-names: Thornton, Hubberston, Stackpole, Templeton, Bosherston, Upton, Castlemartin, Wiston — the 'ton' element meaning town or village. Flemish settlers were introduced to the area around the Cleddau rivers, adding to Pembrokeshire's cultural mix. The imaginary border between the Norman and Welsh dominated territories became known as the *landsker*, marked by a string of castles from **Roch** (133) in the west to **Narberth (49)** in the east. The area south of this line is still known as 'the little England beyond Wales'.

The social changes brought about by the Norman's were paralleled by a change in architecture, and in west Wales (as indeed throughout the rest of the country), the monuments of the Middle Ages continue to dominate the rural landscape. The **castle** is undoubtedly the most familiar of the Norman innovations, and much has been written

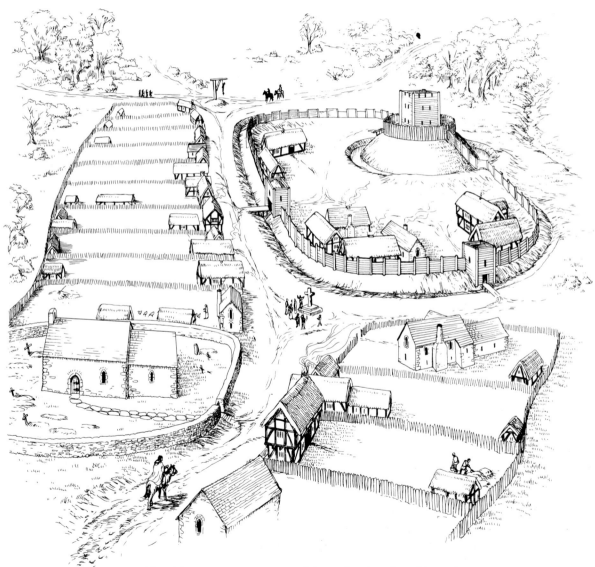

New Moat; an imaginary view of the Medieval castle and borough.

Reconstruction of a Norman earth and timber 'ringwork' castle.

on this subject. The first castles set up were un-sophisticated earthwork fortifications with ditches, wooden towers and encircling stockades. The 'keep' or *Donjon* as it was originally called, contained the main domestic chamber — the hall — within a heavily defended tower on the summit of a steep mound, the *motte*. In the adjoining court-yard, or *bailey*, other buildings stood, such as a chapel, stable, storeroom and garrison quarters. Another castle type favoured by the Normans was the *ringwork*, where the main buildings were encircled by a strong bank and ditch, lacking a motte.

Today these early castles survive only as a grass-grown earthworks, for the timber superstructures have long since decayed. They can be seen all over the country, often in the vicinity of a town or village they once protected, such as **St Clears (33)**, **Templeton (48)**, **New Moat (81)** and **St David's (147)**. Many of the larger and more important earthwork castles were later rebuilt in stone,

usually starting off with a tower or two, a length of curtain wall, finally evolving into massive and elaborate fortresses designed to outwit the most tenacious of enemies. The great castles of **Kid-welly (2)**, **Llansteffan (13)**, **Wiston (55)**, **Manor-bie (96)**, **Carew (99)**, **Pembroke (101)** and **Haver-fordwest (115)** embody work of several periods reflecting the architectural history of Medieval fortress.

The Normans also affected the spiritual as well as the social environment of Wales. The old Celtic religious centres, such as **St Dogmael's (28)** and **Caldey (94)**, were refounded as branches of the European monasteries more familiar to the inva-ders. Many of the small churches and chapels were re-dedicated to 'foreign' saints: St Curig's chapel at **Newport (65)** becme the parish church of St Martin. It was during the Middle Ages that many of the native churches were rebuilt and extended on an impressive scale — **St Mary's Kidwelly (2)**, **St Mary's, Tenby (88)** and **St David's (147)** are noteable examples. However the vast majority of buildings are unsophisticated and lack of the refinement of many English parish churches.

The ecclesiastical buildings which the visitor can explore today are rarely the product of one period of construction; most are culminations of centuries of modification and extension, and few remain as they were first built. It would appear that most early churches comprised a *nave* (where the congregation was seated) and an eastern *chancel* (where the high altar was positioned). In later centuries when money was made available, additions to the fabric would take place — a transept or side chapel was usually built off the nave, linked to the chancel by a *passage-squint*, so that worshippers could still see the altar. Single transept churches include **Carmarthen (16), Gumfreston (90)** and **Henry's Moat (82)**, while **Laugharne (34), Slebech (53), St Florence (91), Pwllchrochan (103), Johnston (118)** and **St Ishmael's (124)** have the more usual twin transepts resulting in a building of *cruciform*

plan. This plan is also reflected in the ruined monastic churches of **St Dogmael's (28), Whitland (31)** and **Pill (121)**. The addition of a *tower* or *aisle* could result in a highly complex structure which can only be understood by a detailed study of the building. **Tenby (88), Manorbier (96), Stackpole (113)** and **St David's (147)** are examples of this.

The churches of west Wales therefore exhibit work of different architectural periods — Norman, Early English, Decorated and Perpendicular. There are few buildings of purely one style. Additions and alterations were also carried out in post-Reformation times. Many carved timber screens and mural decorations did not survive the puritanical zeal of the reformers and iconoclasts, and a particular target was the *rood-loft*, a wooden gallery and crucifix set above the chancel arch. There are no remains of rood images in west Wales today, but their former presence can be detected by *intra-mural* stairs and supporting

Kidwelly Castle; an imposing stone fortress of the 13th century.

15

Eglwys Cymmyn; a 15th century church on a Dark Age site.

corbels (brackets). The well-meaning hand of the Victorian restorer has also modified the appearance of many Medieval churches.

Not all of these religious buildings survived the vicissitudes of the centuries; most of the abbeys were dismantled in the 16th century although some, like **Kidwelly (2), St Clear's (33)** and **Monkton (101)**, survived in parochial use. A number of churches and chapels were abandoned and left to decay, due perhaps to climatic conditions or the depopulation of rural areas. **Capel Dyddgen (7), Llanfihangel Abercywin (15), Llawhaden (52), Slebech (53)** and **St Govans (110)** are now empty, echoing ruins.

One of the less familiar aspects of the Medieval religious world is the devotion attatched to holy wells. From an early age the life-giving qualities and symbolism of running water have been venerated, and it was the policy of the Early Christian Church to sanctify and dedicate such wells in memory of local saints. Sometimes chapels were built on, or near, springs, around which grew a variety of legends and beliefs associated with the healing quality of the water. The remains of well-houses and chapels can be seen at **Llansteffan (13), Higgon's Well (116), Llanllawer (70), Gumfreston (90)** and St Non's (148). Faith in the magical properties of wells still continues today though to a lesser degree, and the bottom of St Non's well still glitters with votive coins from modern pilgrims.

Moving down the architectural scale, the care and expense lavished on castles, churches and abbeys was rarely repeated on the houses of the lower classes. Many Medieval dwellings were simple structures of timber or wattle and daub, and rarely survive in any early form. However, the abundance of stone in parts of the country meant that some houses were built to last. South Pembrokeshire is particularly rich in Medieval stone houses, many of them easily identified by the presence of so-called 'Flemish' *round chimneys* (which have nothing to do with the 12th-century Flemings at all, but are believed to have been copied from contemporary castle architecture). Another common feature is the *vaulted undercroft*, found mainly in upper class houses. The Elizabethan historian George Owen of Henllys

16

bemoaned that 'the workmen of this adge are not soe skillfull, or at least soe carefull as those of the former adges', and also that 'the masons were so skillfull in ould tyme in these countries that most Castells and houses of any accompt were builded with vaultes verye stronglie and substanciallye wrought'. The numerous surviving thick-walled shells bear out Owen's statement. The vaulted chambers were invariably used for storage, and the main domestic chamber — the hall — was located on the floor above. The great ruined mansions of **Court Farm (1)**, **Penallt (4)**, **Boulston (56)**, **Scotsborough (89)** and **Haroldston (117)** are contrasted by the humbler, though no less interesting, dwellings of the minor landowners, at **Templeton (48)**, **Garn (71)**, **Penally (93)**, **Lydstep (95)**, **Monkton (101)** and **Flimston (109)**.

A few of these early buildings bridge the gap between the purely domestic dwelling and the fortified castle; the cramped, multi-storeyed *tower house* at **Angle (106)** has Scottish parallels, but the smaller versions at **Sister's House (47)**, **Carswell (91)** and **Eastington (104)** are more individual. These houses, like the aforementioned castles and churches, need not be all of one build, and reflect the varied and changing architectural personality of this historic landscape.

So far this brief introduction has placed the sites and monuments included here in their proper historical and architectural perspective. However, a great number of these past relics have become emeshed in popular legend and folk-lore which in truth have nothing to do with them, and yet, paradoxically, are integral with their fuller

Garn Farm; a yeoman's hall-house showing a typical Pembrokeshire round chimney.

Johnston parish church.

understanding. For such stories only reflect what the former inhabitants of this land believed the various monuments represented, or what they were used for. It does not matter if King Arthur is not really buried within a stone circle on the Preseli Mountains, or that the ghost of a Welsh princess does not walk down the empty corridors of Carew Castle. These folk-tales simply highlight another facet of the varied role of the ancient monument in the Welsh landscape, and its relationship to Man and the environment.

And so finally to the illustrated gazeteer section. This is arranged into seven geographical areas, with the sites included linked by numbers to the main map. Although this may seem haphazard, the intention is that a visitor staying in a particular place, can glance at the map to find out what monuments are in the immediate vicinity. For the dedicated antiquity hunter, this book should be supplemented by the Ordnance Survey 'Landranger' maps nos. 145, 157, 158 and 159, which indicate all the roads and paths to take in order to reach the sites included. Visitors should also be aware that the majority of the sites mentioned in this book are scheduled Ancient Monuments, and it is an offence to injure or damage them. At the rear of the book is a list of suggested tours, a bibliography and a classified list of the sites and monuments included in the text.

Massive chimney at the Carmarthen Arms, Haverfordwest.

Tenby; the Tudor Merchant's House.

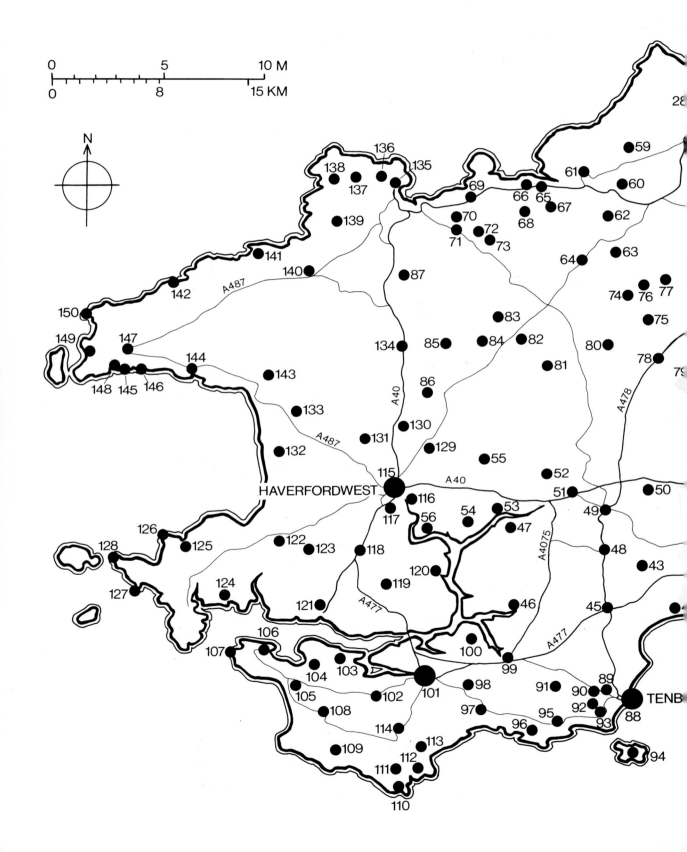

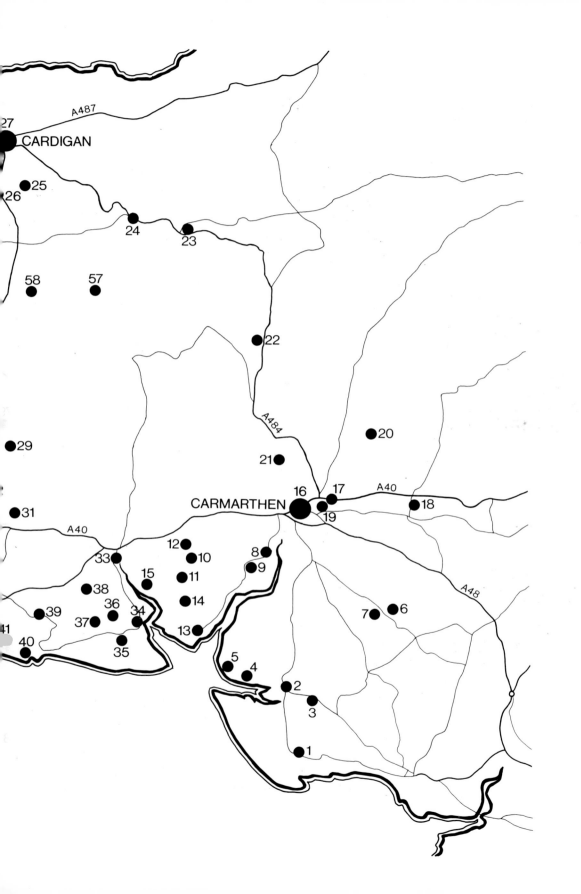

South-West Carmarthenshire

(Sites 1–15)

PEMBREY COURT (1)

Set on a hillside overlooking the bleak expanse of Pembrey Burrows and the Loughor Estuary is Court Farm, the ivy-covered crumbling shell of a once proud mansion. The manor of Pembrey was held by the Butler family from the 14th century to the early 16th, when it passed to the influential Vaughan family. Most of the existing ruin is likely to have been the work of Sheriff Walter Vaughan, although it may incorporate the core of an earlier, semi-fortified manor house. In the 17th century an additional wing was added to the rear, forming a U-shaped range. The earliest surviving masonry is the south wing, which includes a first-floor hall, kitchen, and tower-like porch. A short distance downhill is a large barn, surprisingly provided with a battlemented parapet. It is not clear if this was merely an extravagant decoration or part of the original courtyard wall. The Court was finally

abandoned in 1948, and today the building is in a wretched state. Some of the walls and roofs have fallen, and rats and bats are now the only occupants. The remains of this historic building lie beside the mountain road to Trimsaran, and although a public footpath leads past the house, visitors should not enter the dangerous building.

The modern village of Pembrey clusters about the parish church of St Illtyd at the foot of the hill. Although the church was extensively restored in 1856-7 and 1912, it still retains a number of interesting early features. The nave may be late 13th century in date, but the whole structure was altered in the 14th and 16th centuries when a north aisle, side chapel and a tall, battlemented tower were added. The underside of a 16th-century window arch in the nave is decorated with eight coats of arms, including those of the Butler family, and another bearing the emblems of the Passion. The original door to the church was probably beneath the west window. Beside the window can be seen a straight joint in the masonry which clearly indicates that the tower was added to the earlier nave. Such joints, abutments and changes in stonework, indicate the various phases in the archi-

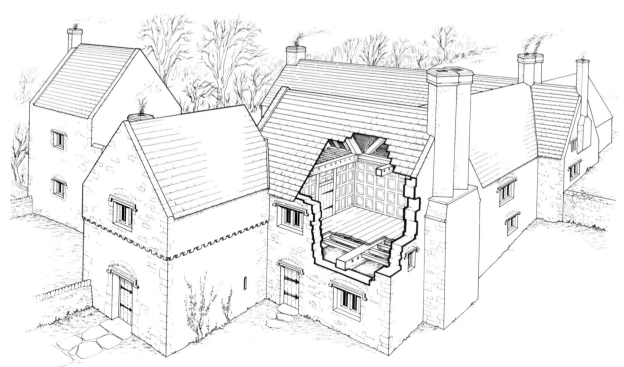

Pembrey; cutaway view of the 16th century court.

22

Kidwelly; the outer gatehouse of the castle.

tectural development of a building. In 1684 the Churchwardens reported that 'the church of Pen-bree is kept in good repaire in all parts, with such cleanlyness, decency, and in good order as becomes the House of God'. Only 13 years earlier the picture was very different: the loft and floor beams had decayed, the windows unglazed, and the chancel screen in need of repair. Worse still, there was no English Bible in the church!

KIDWELLY (2)

On now to the Medieval borough of Kidwelly, first passing the 15th-century **Pont Spwdwr** bridge (3) near Llandyri. The narrow, five-arched bridge is now used by pedestrians, for a new bridge carries the B4308 across the Gwendraeth Fawr river alongside.

The historic town of Kidwelly is still dominated by the ruins of its mighty castle, although the tall spire of the priory church also vies for attention. The origins of the town date back to the beginning of the 12th century, when Henry I granted the surrounding territory to his ambitious minister, Bishop Roger of Salisbury. Roger ordered the building of a castle to defend his hold on the land, and so a large and strong ringwork was constructed on the banks of the tidal river Gwendraeth Fach. Outer enclosures defended the castle's north and south-west flanks, and the latter also sheltered the early town. During the 12th and 13th centuries this foreign plantation was a particular target for Welsh hostility, and it was not until the late 13th century, when conditions had stabilized, that an extensive scheme of rebuilding in stone took place. Between c. 1270 and the early 14th century the castle was rebuilt piecemeal on an imposing scale, and the town enclosed with a protective wall. However, the cramped bailey soon proved inadequate for the growing town, and suburbs developed to the north and south of the old centre. The main area of extra-mural settlement was in the vicinity of the priory church across the river where, until recently, several fine Medieval houses stood.

The mainstay of the economy was a prosperous cloth manufacturing industry, based at several fulling mills on the course of the Gwendraeth. In the early years of the 15th century, Kidwelly was devastated by the Welsh during the national uprising led by Owain Glyndwr. Although the castle was not taken, the gatehouse was burnt and the town razed. This attack checked further development, and in the early 16th century the Tudor antiquarian, John Leland, reported that 'the old town is nere al desolatid', in contrast to the expanding 'new town' across the river.

THE CASTLE

Despite the ravages of war and decay of centuries, the great castle of Kidwelly is substantially intact, and the earthwork defences of the original Norman stronghold form a daunting obstacle even today, some 870 years after they were constructed. The earliest surviving stonework dates to the 1270s when the young Lord Payn de Chaworth began to build the present inner ward — a square enclosure with round towers on the corners — within the pre-existing Norman ringwork. A later owner, Henry, Earl of Lancaster, constructed the outer ward defences in the early 14th century, a curving wall studded with towers, on the line of the old earthworks. At the south end of the enclosure a large and formidable gatehouse was begun, but it may not have been completed until some years after the Glyndwr rebellion. Even in a great military stronghold like this, religious requirements were not neglected, and a two-storey tower containing a chapel was added on the river-side of the inner ward. The castle became Crown property on the accession of the Lancastrian Henry IV in 1399, but it was later granted by Henry VII to the influential Carmarthenshire knight, Sir Rhys ap Thomas, in recognition of services rendered at Bosworth. By then, however, decay appears to have set in, for new buildings were needed, and it was not long before the great fortress was finally abandoned.

Beyond the towering castle gatehouse stands the old town, still partly enclosed by its 13th-century defensive wall, with the ruins of the south gate at the end of Bailey Street. A few old houses survive, such as the 17th-century 'Old Moathouse', while on the riverbank below stands an 1804 cornmill, built on, or near, the site of a Medieval precursor.

THE PRIORY CHURCH OF ST MARY

The castle and church lie across the river from one another, both symbols of the twin powers of the Medieval world, secular and ecclesiastical. This grand, cathedral-like building was originally a Benedictine Priory church, founded by Bishop Roger in 1114 as a dependent cell of Sherborne Abbey, Dorset. From its early days the monastic church also served as the parish church, and this ensured its survival at the Dissolution of the Monasteries in 1539. Most of this cruciform building dates from the 14th century, although the solidly butressed tower was rebuilt in 1481, after it had been struck by lightning and collapsed on the nave. The truncated west end of the church is a relic of that celestial mishap, but the spire was struck again in 1658 and in 1884. The latter event prompted a general restoration of the building under the guidance of Sir George Gilbert Scott, and the existing broach spire is his work.

'This is the House of God, the Gateway of Heaven' proclaims an 18th-century Latin inscription above the door to the tower. The interior of the nave is a vast space with a Victorian waggon roof and numerous memorial tablets on the walls. There are mural passages in the north and south nave walls, one of which led up to anchorite's cell. Another passage in the south-east pier of the crossing led up to the long-vanished rood loft, while repairs to the chancel wall in 1973 revealed a 'squint', used by people in the chantry chapel to catch a glimpse of the altar. There are three Medieval grave slabs in the south transept, but the most interesting stone carving here is a 14th-century alabaster effigy of the Virgin and Child, set on a corbel beside the altar. The stumpy figure (bereft of its lower half) formerly stood in a niche above the door, and the local women used to curtsey to it on entering the church. This so enraged the vicar that he threw the effigy into the churchyard, an action more in keeping with those inconoclasts who wreaked havoc on the monastic glories of this church in the 16th century.

PENALLT (4)

A short drive west along the country road from Kidwelly to St Ishmael's brings the visitor to

Kidwelly; the priory church of St. Mary.

Penallt farm on the coastal plain bordering the Gwendraeth estuary. Below the farm stands the crumbling remains of Penallt, a late Medieval mansion of the Dwnn family. Permission to visit the site must be obtained from the farm, but the remains are visible from the road and railway. The building was once thought to have been a castle or priory, but the remains are those of a large and impressive mansion. The ground floor was divided into vaulted chambers with the great hall, kitchen and other domestic chambers on the first floor. The 15th-century owner of Penallt, John Dwnn, has the distinction of being the first Welshman to have had his portrait painted. This Carmarthenshire landowner can be seen on the 'Chatsworth Triptych' in the National Gallery, painted in 1477.

ST ISHMAEL'S CHURCH (5)

A mile or so beyond Penallt is the impressively sited church of St Ishmael. The saddleback towered building huddles against a steep hillside overlooking the Tywi estuary. On a late summer's evening the rays of the setting sun mellow the rugged stonework of this 13th-14th-century building, but in winter, when fierce storms sweep in across

Penallt; a reconstructed view of the Medieval house.

St. Ishmaels; the parish church.

Carmarthen Bay, the scene is very different. Because of its location, the upper end of the building has been terraced into the hillside, while the opposite end facing the steep slope is propped up with massive butresses. The venerable, ivy-covered building is entered through the vaulted ground floor chamber of the tower. There is no stair to the upper floor, and the only access is by a ladder to an unglazed window. The interior of the church has unfortunately been over-restored, but several post-Medieval memorial stones survive. Prior to the restoration of 1860, there existed a wooden chair, divided down the middle, into which erring couples were made to sit wearing a white cloth over their heads, for the duration of the service. Presumably this embarrassing 'penance' was devised to give married couples second thoughts about quarrelling in future (or at least exercise more discretion over their marital tiffs).

Below the church the hillside slopes down to a level coastal plain ending in a stretch of sand dunes. Hereabouts stood the lost village of Hawton, over-whelmed by the sea during a great storm in 1603. Fragments of Medieval potsherds have been picked up along the beach, and the foundations of buildings observed from time to time.

MYNYDD LLANGYNDEYRN (6)

Around 4000 years ago the bleak limestone ridge of Mynydd Llangyndeyrn, seven miles south-east of Carmarthen, was a focal point of Prehistoric ceremonies and rituals. A public footpath leaves the B4306 road at its highest point between Crwbin and Pontyberem, and from it the numerous ancient monuments can be reached.

The first, and most obvious, monument encountered on the ridge is a 9 feet high standing stone which was excavated in 1976-7. This monolith now stands alone, but excavation revealed that there was originally a timber framed structure (possibly a hut) set against one side of the stone, with a ring-trench a short distance away. These curious features evidently had some ritual function, and presumably marked the approach to the 'sacred'

26

burial ground further along the ridge. Another smaller stone was also excavated further uphill to the north. About 350 yards east of the summit, at the foot of a rock outcrop, are two ruined Neolithic burial chambers of the sub-megalithic type (ie. natural boulders propped up to form makeshift tombs). These chambers are the earliest known sepulchral monuments on the mountain. With the new customs and rituals introduced during the succeeding Early Bronze Age, at least six cairns were built along the ridge, including those of the 'ring' and 'platform' type. The large cairn by the summit of the mountain has been mistakenly described in some old guidebooks as a 'stone circle', although the prominent ring of stones surrounding the mound is only the remains of a kerb. In the *Itinerarium Curiosum* (1725) of the famous antiquarian William Stuckley, there is a sketch of this cairn labelled as 'a Druid Temple'. Stuckley had, in fact, copied it from an earlier drawing, and transformed this modest monument into an elaborate triple concentric ring of stones with a central burial

Mynydd Llangyndeirn standing stone.

chamber. All that can be seen today are the tumbled kerb-stones of the grass-covered mound.

CAPEL DYDDGEN (7)

This is undoubtedly one of the most atmospheric of the many ruined churches in west Wales; with its jagged stumps of masonry, wreathed in ivy and undergrowth, set on a hillside with a spectacular view over the Gwendraeth valley to the distant Preseli Mountains. It is almost to be expected that a religious building should have been established in the vicinity of such an important Prehistoric 'pagan' centre as Mynydd Llangyndeyrn. Capel Dyddgen, or Llanlothegyrn, lies about half a mile west of Crwbin, beside a narrow lane to Felindre. The church may have been built to serve the spiritual needs of an upland community of mill workers, for by 1540 there were no less than 7 mills on the nearby mile-long Drysgeirch stream. But in the post-Medieval period the community declined, and only a few scattered farms remain. By the time the antiquarian Richard Fenton visited Capel Dyddgen in 1804, he saw only 'the ruins of a very neat chapel, the shell pretty entire, a neat tower with battlements, and a handsome archway leading to the chancel'. Today the crumbling 14th-century tower survives almost to parapet height, but the rest of the building has fallen.

A more intact example of a Medieval church lies down in the valley, at the riverside village of Llangyndeirn. The large 13th-14th-century parish church has an unusually tall, thin tower, and is dedicated to the 6th-century St Kentigern, one of the earliest of the Celtic missionaries. When the neglected building was restored in 1883-8 a surprising discovery was made tightly packed beneath — almost 500 skeletons the floor of the nave. All the remains were those of male adults without any apparent wounds, and therefore unlikely to have been casualties of battle. A possible explanation is that the Medieval church was built on top of the graveyard of a Dark Age monastery, although no other evidence, in the form of Early Christian carved stones, survives to support this theory.

Before arriving at the ancient county town of Carmarthen, it is worth exploring the rich legacy of Prehistoric and Medieval sites and monuments in the hill country between the estuaries of the rivers Taf and Tywi. At **Green Castle (8)** the B4312 Car-

Capel Dyddgen.

marthen to Llansteffan road curves past the ivy-covered shell of the hilltop manor house of the Rede family. This is a misnomer, for Green Castle was never a castle, although an 18th-century etching of the ruins shows a crenellated courtyard wall, suggesting that it may have been semi-fortified. In any case its lofty location would have rendered it secure from all but the most determined attacker. Part of the original late Medieval hall survives, incorporated into a range of Tudor buildings which include a tall, many-windowed stair tower.

About 1½ miles further along the road is the first of several megalithic monuments in this area. **Myrddin's Quoit (9)** is a group of three standing stones (*leaning* might be a better word) in a field on

the left of the road near Llwyn-du farm. The site has nothing to do with Myrddin (or Merlin), and it is all that remains of what was once described as '*a perfect cromlech*'. Three miles further west, in a valley below Llangynog schoolhouse, is another ruined Neolithic burial chamber, **Twlc y Filiast (10)** (*'Kennel of the greyhound bitch'*). This name too, derives from Arthurian legend, and is believed to be an allusion to the King's wild boar hunt re-counted in 'The Mabinogion'. Leaving the realms of fantasy for fact, excavations here in 1953 uncovered several interesting features relating to the construction and use of the tomb. The burial chamber itself was built of local glacial boulders set upright in pits dug into the ground. An oval cairn mound 60 feet long was then heaped around the chamber. A capstone measuring 8 feet long was probably obtained from the nearby boulder-strewn slopes, and dragged along on rollers (using the cairn as a ramp) to be set into place above the chamber. In front of the main chamber there was a smaller and lower 'antechamber', which had received a dedicatory cremation burial before construction. Excavation also uncovered the remains of a kerbed *forecourt* and entrance passage leading from the south edge of the cairn towards the burial chamber.

Moving through the centuries we arrive at the less enigmatic monuments of the Iron Age. **Castell Cogan (11)** occupies the summit of an isolated hill beside the Llangynog to Pentrenewydd road. The defences of this small hillfort consist of a bivallate inner enclosure with a larger outer enclosure on the north and west sides. The outer defences are poorly preserved, but the inner rampart survives to a height of 14 feet. Excavations in 1971 uncovered the foundations of two round huts within the inner enclosure, marked by concentric rings of post-holes. Both huts had been burnt down and the defences razed, perhaps due to a deliberate policy of demilitarization by the invading Romans.

Further to the north-east are two more Iron Age settlements. The roadside site at **Bwlch y Seiri (12)**, west of Llangynog, is a ploughed-down univallate enclosure with an annexe on the west side. Less than a third of a mile away, on the opposite side of the valley, is a 1st-2nd century Romano-British settlement known simply as 'Llangynog II'. This survives today as a bank and ditch enclosure with a causewayed entrance on the east side. Excavations in 1972 and 1974 revealed

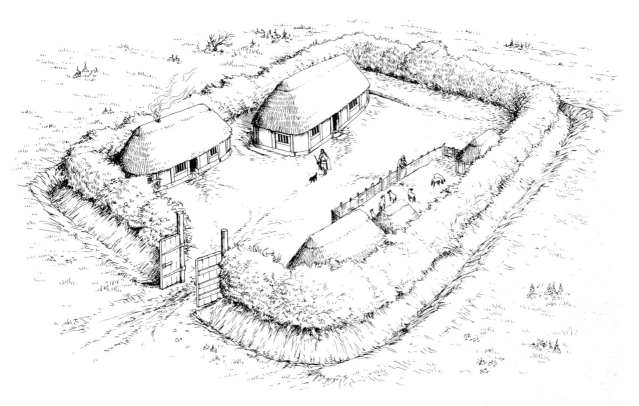

Llangynog; reconstruction of the Romano-British settlement.

that the settlement was surrounded only by a shallow ditch, and possibly an inner hedge. Two levelled platforms in the interior marked the site of timber buildings, the larger of which had a ditch on the uphill side to carry away excess rainwater. A number of post-holes at the entrance revealed that the timber gate had been remodelled on four different occasions, and the evidence also suggests that the main building was disused and partially dismantled at the time it was burnt down. An interesting, though unproven, theory is that this undefended farmstead was a successor to the nearby fortified Bwlch y Seiri enclosure, a change of site perhaps dictated by the Roman overseers at Carmarthen.

LLANSTEFFAN (13)

Llansteffan castle is one of several Iron Age hillforts in west Wales which was taken over and adapted for use by the Norman invaders (see also 61, 122 and 129). The 12th-century stronghold consisted of an earth and timber ringwork shelter-ing in one corner of the long-abandoned multi-vallate hillfort. The deep ditches and strong ramparts of this Prehistoric fortress still survive on the north and west sides of the later stone castle.

Contemporary chronicles record that Llansteffan was captured by the Welsh in 1146, 1189, 1215 and 1257, and it was after the final raid that the old defences were rebuilt in stone on an extensive scale. The Norman ringwork had already received some stonework, in the form of a crude encircling wall with two towers, but now the remainder of the castle was enclosed with a tall curtain wall with flanking towers and a large, three-storey gatehouse. This gatehouse dates from the 1280s and shows the increased concern for the effective defence of the entrance (generally the most vulnerable part of a castle). Although the Great Gatehouse was converted into a residential block in Tudor times (when the entrance was sealed and a new gate constructed alongside), much of the original arrangement can still be traced. The approach was flanked by two half-round towers with strategically placed loop-holes, for the archers' covering fire. Directly above the entrance arch is a chute through which water could be poured to prevent the gates being burnt, or less harmless liquids tipped on any undesirable visitor. There were two portcullises and stout wooden gates, more loop-holes sweeping the entrance passage, and 'murder holes' in the vault above the dropping missiles on any attacker who had got that far. The first and second floors were more amenable chambers stretching the width of the gatehouse, and provided with fireplaces, large win-

dows overlooking the courtyard, and 'hole-in-the-floor' privies (mod.cons. to the Medieval Man, but unacceptable by today's standards). Excavations within the courtyard have revealed the foundations of several buildings, including a small early 13th-century round keep.

At the beginning of the 15th century the castle was occupied for a time by the Welsh under Owain Glyndwr, but this marked its last use as a military stronghold, and although part of the castle was used as a residence in the late 15th century, it was soon left to decay.

Llansteffan; cutaway view through the gatehouse of the castle.

The Medieval parish church and modern villge of Llansteffan lies some distance away from the castle, in a more sheltered position above the Tywi estuary. The church is an imposing cruciform building dating from the 13th-14th century, with a three-storey battlemented tower at the west end. The vaulted ground floor of the 15th-century tower was formerly used as a porch.

A more unusual survivor of the Medieval faith is St Anthony's Holy Well, which lies beyond the castle on the north side of a valley leading down to Scott's Bay. The well has been restored several times and consists of a masonry arch with a recess at the rear that reputedly once held a figure of the saint. Not only are the trickling waters esteemed for healing, but also for fulfilling wishes by throwing in a pin or white quartz pebble.

In contrast to St Stephen's church at Llansteffan, which is still used for regular worship, there are three other religious buildings in this small area of west Wales which have not survived the centuries unscathed. The hilltop village of **Llanybri (14)** is clustered about the gutted shell of a 14th-century church, which lies in the middle of the green. This was originally a chapel-of-ease to Llansteffan, which passed to the Nonconformists in the 17th century. In 1879 the building was thoroughly restored, and most of the surviving Medieval masonry is confined to the stumpy tower (reduced in height in the 19th century) and the chancel walls.

Llansteffan; St. Anthony's well.

About two miles west of Llanybri are two substantial ruined churches, both within sight of each other on opposite banks of the little river Cywin. The first reached is St Teilo's church at **Llandeilo Abercywin (15)**. A public footpath passes through the adjacent farm (which includes a fine Medieval first-floor hall, now modernized) to the church, lying forlorn in an empty graveyard beside the river. The roofless building is a simple rectangular structure with an undivided chancel and nave, and a porch on the south side. The original entrance was through a pointed doorway (later blocked) in the west wall, and the unplastered wall surfaces reveal other modifications to the fabric, notably an eastward extension to the chancel of c. 1500 date. Huge buttresses support the crumbling walls, which had begun to lean long before the church was abandoned earlier this century.

The larger and undoubtedly the most evocative of the two churches here is St Michael's at **Llanfihangel Abercywin**, which lies only a third of a mile away, but can only be reached along a 2½ mile loop of country road. A public footpath leaves the road at Trefenty farm and passes through the yard to the riverside church. The building is substantially intact; the north wall has gone, but the doorways, windows and round-headed chancel arch survive, overlooked by the owl-haunted tower. Llanfihangel Abercywin was founded in the late 11th or early 12th century when the Normans established a large earthwork castle on the hill to the west. This formed a link between the motte and bailey at St Clears (33) and the ringwork at Laugharne (34), and it may have been the castle of 'Aber Cofwy' mentioned in the Chronicles in 1116. The church was built to serve the spiritual needs of the Norman lords and, presumably, the inhabitants of an adjoining settlement. All that now remains of the Medieval foundation (apart from the church) is the overgrown castle mound and the large, rambling 17th-century Trefenty. In the post-Medieval period ther was a gradual shift in population to the north part of the parish where, in the 19th century, a tasteless new church was built.

Within the overgrown churchyard are tombstones of several periods, including the famous 'pilgrim's graves' of 12th or early 13th century date. These are said to commemorate pilgrims who died here on their way to, or from, St David's. Six gravestones survive, three set into concrete beside the church, and the rest hidden by the long grass and weeds. When one of the graves was opened in 1838, half a dozen cockleshells were found beside the skeleton, indicating perhaps that the pilgrim had made the long journey to Compostela in Spain, where shell badges were worn by visitors to the shrine of St James.

Llandeilo Abercywyn; the ruined church of St. Teilo.

Carmarthen and the Teifi Valley

(Sites 16–28)

CARMARTHEN (16)

Alone of the historic towns of west Wales, Carmarthen is unique in that it owes its origins not to the Normans, but to invaders of a far earlier age — the Romans. Just over 2000 years ago the Roman army established a military base here, on a farily level ridge bordering the tidal reaches of the river Tywi. The exact position and extent of this Auxiliary fort has yet to be determined, but it probably stood in the area now occupied by modern King Street, and Spilman Street. To the east a small settlement, or *vicus*, grew up, which in time developed into the *Civitas* capital of the ruling Iron Age tribe of west Wales, the *Demetae*. This Romano-British town was known as *Moridunum* (the 'sea fort'), and functioned in much the same way as a modern county town; the administrative and political centre of a reorganized tribal territory. There were shops, houses, public buildings such as the market (*forum*) and county hall (*basilica*),

all arranged on a grid pattern divided up by broad streets, and enclosed with earthwork defences. Just outside the town to the east stood an **amphitheatre**, cut into the hillside and ringed with wooden tiered seating for perhaps as many as 5000 spectators. This was probably used for military displays, shows and public ceremonies. To date about half the amphitheatre has been excavated and opened to the public, while *Moridunum* itself lies below ground, receiving piecemeal excavation as more of modern Carmarthen is being re-developed. However, the line of the defences has been fossilized by latter-day streets and property boundaries, which define a rectangular area of about 450 × 550 yards.

Several excavations have already taken place within the area of the Roman town, including a section cut through the defences which revealed that the town of c. 200 AD was protected by an earthen rampart and two outer ditches. Then in the late 3rd century these defences were replaced (and partly overlain) by a stone wall with one or more outer ditches. Excavations carried out by the Dyfed Archaeological Trust in Priory Street in 1980-4 uncovered a T-junction of roads flanked by timber buildings, which had been modified and

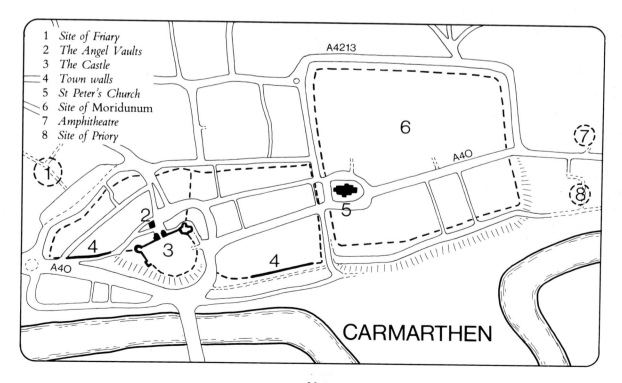

1 Site of Friary
2 The Angel Vaults
3 The Castle
4 Town walls
5 St Peter's Church
6 Site of Moridunum
7 Amphitheatre
8 Site of Priory

CARMARTHEN

rebuilt on a number of occasions. Part of the foundation wall of a Roman temple was also unearthed.

The fate of *Moridunum* in the Dark Ages is uncertain. It undoubtedly declined following the collapse of Roman authority in Britain, but it may be that a small native settlement survived, grouped around the Celtic church of St Teulyddog. The next phase in Carmarthen's history is heralded by the arrival of the Normans in the early 12th century. A castle had already been established in the vicinity in 1093, known as Rhyd y gors, but this may not have been on the site of the later castle and was, in any case, short lived. About 1109 a royal castle was built on the command of Henry I, by Walter of Gloucester. This was a large and strong motte and bailey at the south-western tip of the ridge, some distance from the site of *Moridunum*. Why the Normans chose to ignore the surviving defences of the Roman town is not clear (the castles of Cardiff, Caerleon, Caerwent and Loughor are all situated within Roman works). One theory is that the invaders did not want unnecessarily to alienate the native community by buidling a castle on their doorsteps, but it may be simply that the steep-sided end of the ridge proved more attractive for defence.

Throughout the Middle Ages Carmarthen therefore developed as a dual town — 'old' and 'new' Carmarthen, the former coming under the control of the Augustinian Priory of St John. The Norman plantation borough grew up in the shadow of the royal fortress, defended on its north and west sides by a stream valley and a marsh. Around 1223 the town was surrounded by a wall with four gates, but the area enclosed was small, and extra-mural suburbs soon developed to the east and west. The walled town was provided with its own church, St Mary's, while the inhabitants of the old town were served by St Peter's. Around the middle of the 13th century a second monastic House was founded here, a Franciscan Friary, on land to the west of the castle. In the 1340s plague devastated Carmarthen, and so too did Glyndwr in the early 15th century. Following the uprising a much larger section of the town was encircled with defensive walls, extending the area of new Carmarthen eastwards to within a few yards of the old centre. Much of the castle was also rebuilt at this time.

Carmarthen; a Roman altar in the church porch.

During the post-Medieval period Carmarthen was the most populous town in Wales, and many fine 18th and early 19th-century houses were built. Unlike some of the other towns we shall be discussing later on, Carmarthen has a paucity of early domestic buildings, although two vaulted cellars remain under the Ex-servicemen's Club in Bridge Street, and many other brick-faced vaults may be Medieval in origin. Renovation work on the Angel Vaults Public House in Nott's Square revealed a plastered-over 15th century window on the first floor. The upper floor was also found to have been built projecting out over the street, a feature indicative of a Medieval date. Many other early buildings may still survive, hidden by modern rendering and wall surfaces.

The Castle is the main surviving relic of Carmarthen's Norman heritage. It lies behind Nott's Square, partly obscured by modern shops and houses which preserve the narow, twisting street pattern of the Medieval town. The castle and the adjoining settlement frequently suffered from Welsh raids in the 12th and early 13th centuries, and it was not until 1223 that the English hold was more firmly consolidated when Earl William Marshal II rebuilt the castle in stone. The Earl evidently did a good job, for Carmarthen endured a prolonged three-month siege in 1233. Further costly repairs were carried out when the castle was recovered from the Glyndwr rebels, and a large sum was spent on rebuilding the gatehouse, now the principal feature of the ruins. The Civil War wrought further havoc on the old fortress, and with the conclusion of hostilities it was partly demolished by Cromwell's Roundheads. (Part of the earthwork defences thrown up by the towns-people during that turbulent period can still be seen today, at the rear of the old Police Station.)

Further modifications to the castle precinct in the 18th and 20th centuries has not helped to preserve any archaeological deposits, but work is in progress restoring the overgrown and crumbling walls. Apart from the early 15th-century gate-house, all that survives is a length of curtain wall with two flanking towers, and a hexagonal *shell-keep* on the summit of the early motte. This keep was a remarkable structure with projecting turrets on at least two of the corners, but it is uncertain whether there was lean-to buildings ranged against the inner walls, or if the whole keep was roofed over in the manner of a large tower. The castle was originally divided into an outer and inner ward, the latter referred to in Medieval documents as the *Donjon*, and containing five towers, the keep (*Magna Turris*), a hall, chapel, kitchen and stable. The interior of the castle is now occupied by the County Hall.

St Peter's Church is the parish church of Carmarthen, and may occupy the site of St Teulyddog's Dark Age cell. As might be expected, the building has been thoroughly restored on several occasions, but nevertheless it retains many features of interest. The first of these is a small Roman altar in the porch, a reminder of Carmarthen's pre-Christian past. The church consists of a chancel, nave, a north transept and a long south aisle, with a lofty battlemented tower on the west side. The masonry is probably 13th-15th century in date, with a liberal amount of Victorian work. The lower half of the north nave wall is believed to incorporate the remains of an earlier church, and retains four arched recesses with carved Medieval gravestones. Another finely carved stone in the south chancel bears the coat of arms of the Prince of Wales, and was brought from the vicinity of the priory.

Among the wall tablets and memorial slabs, which are too numerous to list, are three which deserve to be singled out. The most impressive is the early 16th-century altar-tomb of Sir Rhys ap Thomas, the 'Eagle of Carmarthen', one of the un-scrupulous gentry who turned against Richard III to help the usurper Henry Tudor win the Crown of England at Bosworth in 1485. Rhys had sworn an oath to King Richard that no one ill-opposed to the state would ever cross his lands, except over his body; and so, according to legend, Rhys hid under Mullock bridge, Dale, as Henry rode over, and so absolving himself of his oath. In return for his help, Henry rewarded Rhys with large estates in west

Carmarthen; outer gatehouse of the castle.

Carmarthen; the parish church of St. Peter.

Wales, and later made him a Knight of the Garter. Rhys died in 1525 and was laid to rest at the Grey Friars church. At the Dissolution of the Monasteries the tomb was removed to St Peter's, where it suffered heavy 'restoration' in 1865.

On the south wall of the church there is a plaque commemorating the Protestant Bishop of St David's, Robert Ferrar, who was burnt at the stake in front of the castle in 1555. Another notable 'resident' of the church is Walter Devereux (d. 1576), first Earl of Essex, and father of the better-known Essex, Queen Elizabeth's favourite courtier. The exact location of his grave is unknown, but in 1804 his remarkable coffin was unearthed, a curious contraption made of oak bound with iron straps, *'cubiform'* in shape, and *'pointed at both extremities'*. The interior was lined with lead, 'in which the body lay embalmed in a curious sort of spirituous liquor, that had retained its purity in an astonishing manner, and was scarcely diminished in quantity since the time the body was enclosed . . .' Clearly the worthy Earl had been pickled in a 'bottle'!

THE MONASTIC HOUSES

All that survives of the Augustinian priory is part of the precinct enclosure and a fragment of the church itself, embedded in a modern boundary wall. Excavations by the Dyfed Archaeological Trust in 1979 recovered part of the plan of the church, chapter house and Prior's dwelling.

The excavations carried out by the Trust at the Grey friary (and which are still continuing in advance of re-development) have unearthed much of the layout of this, one of the largest Franciscan Houses in Britain. It was initially built along the usual lines, a large church with an adjoining cloister flanked by buildings (chapter house, dormitory, kitchen, etc.). In the late 13th-early 14th century a second cloister was added, again with its own range of buildings, including an infirmary. A large number of skeletons were unearthed beneath the chapter house floor — the mortal remains of the Friars who lived and died in this sumptuous monastery. There were many polished and decorated floor tiles, richly coloured glass windows (one of which was discovered almost in its entirety, and is due to be reconstructed) and the presence of a brewhouse for cider-making suggests that the Friars were not strict teetotallers. When the House was closed at the Dissolution an attempt was made to convert the buildings into a cathedral (to replace St David's), this failed, and although a grammar school was set up in the precinct, this had closed by 1547. Decay, and the inevitable stone robbing, have taken their toll, and nothing now survives of the Friary above the ground.

Leaving Carmarthen for a brief detour along the Tywi valley, a journey of about 1½ miles brings the visitor to the little village of **Abergwili (17)**. There was once an ecclesiastical college here, founded by Bishop Bek of St David's in 1287, but all that now survives of the associated buildings is the impressive post-Medieval Bishop's Palace. Since 1978 the Palace has been the headquarters of the **Carmarthen Museum**, and contains an impressive and varied collection of artifacts reflecting the culture and society of old Carmarthenshire. The groundfloor history and archaeology gallery is particularly relevant to this book, and includes finds from Coygen Cave (35), Prehistoric stone and metal implements, Bronze Age funerary urns, and relics of the Roman occupation of Carmarthenshire. There is also a fine collection of Early

Christian memorial stones, including those from Llanfihangel Croesfeini (21) and the *Voteporix* stone from Castell Dwyran. The latter commemorates the 6th-century 'Protector' who was castigated by the chronicler Gildas as the 'tyrant of Dyfed'. The Palace is also the base of the Dyfed Archaeologial Trust and the Sites and Monuments Record, which stores details and information on all the archaeological remains in west Wales.

In view from the extensive grounds of the Museum are the wooden slopes of **Merlin's Hill**, in legend the site of the wizard's last resting place. The 10-acre summit is encircled with a single massive rampart which curves out on the north-east side to protect the inturned entrance. This is one of the largest Iron Age hillforts in south Wales, and yet it was only 'discovered' in the early 1950s.

NANTGAREDIG HENGE (18)

Continuing along the A40 past the Museum, the small village of Nantgaredig is soon reached. Part of the village has recently been found to lie within the earthwork remains of a Prehistoric henge, rather like a scaled-down version of the better known Avebury in Wiltshire. Little remains to be seen today and much of the site has been built over. At the rear of Ty Coedlan and Clunview houses, Station Road, are two rugged monoliths side by side, the tallest 6feet high. These stones are set at the entrance of an oval earthwork enclosure, 250feet across, with a sunken central area in which several houses have been built. Excavation by the Dyfed Archaeological Trust revealed that there was an internal ditch (or pit) separated from the outer bank by a sloping terrace. Another standing stone in a field 300 yards to the north-west is probably connected with the henge, and may be the sole remnant of a more elaborate megalithic structure.

LLANGUNNOR CHURCH (19)

This small, much restored Medieval church lies amongst a cluster of ancient yews near the summit of Llangunnor hill, about a mile east of Car-

Nantgaredig henge; two standing stones at the entrance to the henge.

Llangunnor; the Dark Age stone.

marthen. From the churchyard there is an uninterrupted view along the meandering course of the river Tywi, past the Welsh strongholds of Dryslwyn and Carreg Cennen, to a backdrop of Foel Fawr and the Black Mountain. Indeed, this splendid viewpoint is the best attraction of Llangunnor, for while there are many other less modernized churches in west Wales, few are so superbly sited. The church is basically two buildings of almost equal length, side by side; the arcade between the two halves was replaced in the early 19th century by an incongruous series of Classical pillars. In the porch is a small 7th-9th century cross stone, which indicates that the hilltop church may occupy the site of a pre-Norman burial ground.

MEINI GWYN (20)

The aptly named Meini Gwyn ('white stones') are three large standing stones on high ground six miles

north-east of Carmarthen. Two can be seen beside the road from Rhydargaeau to Capel Gwyn, while a third lies nearby in the garden of Dolgwm House. All are quartz-veined boulders up to 7feet high, although only two remain upright today. There is a belief that rainwater drawn from a crevice in the top of the Dolgwm stone can be used to cure warts — a curious tradition more commonly associated with holy wells.

LLANFIHANGEL CROESFEINI (21)

This intriguing, but little-known, Dark Age and Medieval site lies on private land about three miles north-west of Carmarthen, just off a minor road from Ffynnon-ddrain to Newchurch. The place-name means 'the church of St Michael of the cross stones', and although nothing survives above ground of the church, the two stones (of 5th to early 6th-century date) can be seen at the Carmarthen Museum. Both stones commemorate important Dark Age figures, namely *Severinus, son of Severus* and *Cunegnus*. In the Middle Ages the Normans established a large ringwork castle beside the Dark Age burial ground, and the chapel was presumably built (or rebuilt) at the same time. Some vague earthworks (of a settlement?) remain between the castle and church site.

In the post-Reformation period the church was abandoned and eventually dismantled, and the stones used to build a nearby barn. The inscribed stones nearly met with a similar fate before they were moved for safety, first to Trawsmawr House, and then to the Museum. On the nearby mountain summit are the burial mounds of people who lived and died in this area 2000 years before the advent of Christianity.

CLAWDD MAWR (22)

Four miles north of Cynwyl Elfed on the left-hand side of the A484 to Llangeler is Clawdd Mawr, a linear earthwork of uncertain age and function. The 'clawdd' is a single bank about 6feet high, and over a mile long, which crosses a prominent east-west ridge between the Tywi and Teifi valleys. The north end of the dyke has been destroyed, but the lower section is preserved as a grassed-over bank partly overlain by a modern hedge. The earthwork may have served some defensive purpose, or else functioned as an upland boundary marker. Its age is uncertain too; the 8th and 9th centuries witnessed a considerable amount of dyke building (eg. Offa's Dyke), and it may be that Clawdd Mawr belongs to that period of history.

The same mountain ridge is dotted with the burial mounds of the Prehistoric tribes of the Tywi and Teifi valleys. The existence of these mounds here is due as much to the Bronze Age predilection for high ground, as to the fact that the uplands have suffered less agricultural activity than the more fertile, low-lying areas. At least three dozen cairns and barrows can be found in the uplands between Llanfyrnach and Pencader. To enumerate them all is beyond the scope of this book, and in any upland area a detailed OS map is essential to locate such monuments. Particularly noteworthy cairns are: Crug yr Ast (beside the B4333 north of Hermon), a group of three mounds on the summit of Moelfre (just off the B4333) and Crug Wen and Crug Perfa, both on open moorland beside a minor road from Clawdd Mawr to Cwmpengraig.

NEWCASTLE EMLYN (23)

The riverside town of Newcastle Emlyn developed from a Medieval settlement which grew up in the shadow of a native Welsh stronghold. The 'New Castle' itself was built around 1240 by Maredudd ap Rhys, on a well-defended hill within an S-bend of the river Teifi. Most of the existing masonry, however, dates to the early 14th century when the castle was in English hands. Around the same time a small town was established on the ridge to the west, which was served by a chapel (since destroyed) at the castle gates. Both town and castle suffered damage in 1403 during the Glyndwr rebellion, but the war-worn stronghold was later rebuilt as a country retreat by Sir Rhys ap Thomas. The extent of Rhys' work here is uncertain, but most of his grandiose architectural ideas were lavished on Carew Castle (99).

Only jagged stumps of masonry and half-buried foundations survive of the castle today — all the result of Roundhead cannonfire when Newcastle Emlyn was garrisoned for the King during the Civil War. A large earthwork bailey defended the more vulnerable western approach to the inner ward, which is dominated by the remains of an early 14th-century gatehouse. The rest of the ward is buried under centuries of debris, although part of a corner tower survives, and excavations are uncovering more of the plan.

Newcastle Emlyn; the castle gatehouse.

CENARTH (24)

Cenarth is a pleasant village on the banks of the Teifi, a place more renowned for its salmon and cascades than any historic monument. There are, nevertheless, two sites worthy of attention; on private land but visible from the roadside, is a tree-covered motte. This lies in a field opposite the parish church, and may have been the 'old' castle of Emlyn which the previous site (23) was meant to replace.

Although the church of St Llawddog is modern, it contains a relic of its Medieval predecessor — a remarkably pagan-looking font. On the side of the stone bowl are carved five crude human heads enclosed within a serpentine moulding. The blank, staring faces are similar to many Iron Age cult images, for the severed head (preferably an enemy's) was revered by the ancient Celts. Just outside the church door is another carved stone, this one far older and not an original feature of early Cenarth. This is the 'Gellidywyll Stone', a 5th or early 6th-century Latin memorial slab, commemorating *Curcagnus, son of Andagellus*. The stone has been moved around the country several times, and was originally at Llandeilo (80), where two stones commemorate other members of the same family.

Just over 800 years ago the celebrated cleric and chronicler, Gerald of Wales, passed through Cenarth on a tour of the country. Gerald reported that there was a *'flourishing fishing station'* here, and he was evidently impressed with the local wildlife. He devoted a large section of his book *The Journey Through Wales*, to the habits of the Cenarth salmon and beavers: 'Of all the rivers in Wales, and of those in England south of the Humber, it is the only one where you can find beavers.' The salmon and their human predators are still at Cenarth, but the beavers, alas, have gone.

CILGERRAN (25)

Cilgerran castle has long attracted the attention of the sightseer and Romantic artist, and it is not hard to see why; the castle is perched on the edge of a wooded gorge with the Teifi flowing turgidly at its foot. Cilgerran castle was not founded for any aesthetic reasons, however, but as an outpost of Norman authority and a symbol of foreign over-lordship. It may have been established as early as

1108 by Gerald of Windsor, castellan of Pembroke, as a stronghold in which to keep his family and possessions safe. If so, he failed, for in 1109 the Welsh lord Owain ap Cadwgan broke into Gerald's castle and kidnapped his beautiful wife, Nest. In the confusion Gerald was forced to escape through the privy drains (a rare example of a Norman covering himself in something other than glory).

The existing masonry, however, was not added to the site until 1223 when Earl William Marshall II began to 'build an ornate castle of mortar and stones' as the contemporary chronicles put it. This 'ornate' structure consisted of most of the inner ward; a strong curtain wall and gatehouse isolating the end of the sheer-sided promontory site. Unlike his father, who had built a huge keep at Pembroke (101), Marshal opted for two large round towers projecting out from the wall, providing added defence for the vulnerable southern approach.

Cilgerran; the castle.

These towers also functioned as self-contained keeps, capable of being held even if the rest of the castle had fallen to an enemy. Later in the 13th century the remainder of the inner and outer wards were refortified in stone. Much of this later work is now very ruinous, but the Earl Marshal's lofty battlements and towers still survive relatively intact.

Beyond the castle gates stood the Medieval town, which may have replaced an earlier Welsh settlement in the vicinity of the parish church. The church bears a dedication to St Llawddog, and has a 6th-century inscribed stone in the graveyard. The Latin and Ogham inscription commemorates one *Trenagustus* or *Trenegussus*.

Another stone of similar age is kept at nearby **Bridell Church** (26), just over a mile to the south-west. This has only an Ogham inscription which reads 'NETTASAGRU MAQI MUCOI BRECI' = *Nettasagrus, son of the descendant of Brecos*. The latter name has been interpreted as Brychan, the Dark Age king of Brecon. A cross was later carved on one side of the stone some three centuries after it had been set up in memory of this otherwise unknown person.

CARDIGAN (27)

The Teifi-side town of Cardigan owes it origins to the entrepreneurial activites of the Norman land-grabbers in the late 11th century. In 1093 Earl Roger of Montgomery arrived at the broad estuary of the river and constructed an earth and timber fort to guard a bridge-head route into native territory. This fortress was apparently abandoned after a Welsh uprising in 1094, and the next attempt at re-colonizing Cardigan occurred in 1110, when Henry I granted the territory to Earl Gilbert fitz Richard. The importance attached to Cardigan as a strategic base is indicated by its frequent capture and destruction recorded in the contemporary chronicles. Betwen 1171 and 1197 it was in the hands of the Lord Rhys of Deheubarth, who rebuilt the timber defences in stone and later held a great contest here between bards and musicians (a forerunner of the present-day Eisteddfod). The English hold on Cardigan was not fully consolidated until the second quarter of the 13th century, when the castle was again rebuilt, and the adjacent town defended by a stone wall and gates. In the later Middle Ages the town suffered a

St. Dogmael's; the remains of the north transept.

Cardigan; the priory church.

decline, in common with many other Welsh boroughs, and there is now, sadly, little above-ground evidence of its Medieval heritage.

The interior of the castle was turned into the garden of a Georgian mansion (now in gloomy decay), which incorporates the remains of a 13th-century keep. The rest of the defensive circuit is farily intact, although the walls have been patched up and are now in an alarmingly insecure state. Along with the town and castle Earl Gilbert also founded a Benedictine Priory on the riverbank a short distance upstream. All that now remains of this establishment is the 14th-century pinnacled chancel of the monastic church of St Mary's. The rest of the building was practically rebuilt at the beginning of the 18th century.

ST DOGMAEL'S ABBEY (28)

St Mary's was not the only monastic house on this stretch of the Teifi: more substantial work survives of St Dogmael's Abbey, a mile further downriver. This House of Tironian monks was founded by Robert fitz Martin around 1113 on, or near, the site of a Celtic monastery of which several Early Christian stones survive. The most important of these pre-Norman relics is the *Sagrani* stone, now kept in the Victorian parish church. The bi-lingual Latin and Ogham inscription enabled historians to decipher the enigmatic Irish runic script.

Since 1947 excavations have revealed virtually all of the ground plan of the Abbey — from the original early 12th-century church, to the great ovens and kitchens of a post-Reformation house built over part of the west range. The surviving masonry belongs to almost every period of Medieval building — the small and austere Norman work with apsidal chapels and chancel; the 13th-century nave walls and vaulted Presbytery crypt; a 14th-century Chapter House and Abbot's guest chambers; and finally the disproportionately large north transept, once roofed over with a finely decorated vault. This transept was rebuilt in the early 16th century, and represents the last work undertaken before the Dissolution put paid to the faded glories of the monasteries. On the east side of the cloister stands a 13th-century Infirmary, one of the few buildings here to survive relatively intact. It was built to house the infirm and elderly brethren, but is now used as a storeroom for the many carved stones and sculptured effigies found during excavations.

West Carmarthenshire and the Cleddau

(Sites 29–56)

LLANBOIDY (29)

Huddled away in the rolling hills north of Whitland is the little village of Llanboidy, strung out along a low ridge between two tributaries of the Gronw river. There was some kind of settlement here at least 1400 years ago, for set into the wall of the much-restored Medieval parish church is a 6th-century memorial slab to *Mavohenus, son of Lunarchus Coccus*. The stone was apparently once set into the bellcot, but during restoration work it was removed and built into the blocked doorway in the south wall of the nave. A second stone here is now lost, but the inscription was fortunately recorded in the 18th century, and commemorated *Echadus, son of Itocus*. Whether there was a native settlement at Llanboidy by the time the Normans arrived here is uncertain, but a motte and bailey castle was built by the invaders to keep a watchful eye on the district. The grass-covered, 20 foot high mound, with its adjoining bailey, can be seen in a field south-east of the village, beside the road to Whitland.

About half a mile south of Llanboidy, and just within sight of the road, is a large and impressive promontory fort, Hafod Camp. The artificial defences were massed on the level north approach — an outer bank and ditch with a much more powerful inner rampart and ditch. The remainder of the 5 acre enclosure was adequately defended by the natural slopes, but just to be sure the hillfort builders scarped and steepened the hillside. Some Roman coins were allegedly found within the fort around 1800, which suggests that this Iron Age settlement was in use during the Roman period.

LLANBOIDY BARROWS (30)

More relics of Prehistoric Man can be found in the hills west of Llanboidy. At the mountain-top road junctions of Lan and Crosshands (respectively 1¼ and 1½ miles west and north-west of the village) are two groups of Early Bronze Age burial mounds. Two of the mounds at Lan were excavated in 1929 and found to contain a central cremation burial covered over with a cairn of white quartz stones, which in turn was encased in a mound of clay.

The Crosshands group is larger and more complex. There is also a totally ruined Neolithic tomb here, which predates the barrows by at least a thousand years. One urn burial was discovered in 1920 when one of the mounds was destroyed by ploughing, but more information was obtained by the excavation of two barrows a few year later. Both had internal stone settings which were concealed within the covering mound; in one of the barrows there was a ring-cairn of quartz pebbles, and in the other a diminutive 'stone circle' surrounding the central burial. All the burial urns belong to the later phase of the Early Bronze Age, and represent the cemetery of the tribe which lived in this area around 3000 years ago.

WHITLAND (31)

There are no surviving relics of Whitland's renowned heritage, only a memorial garden commemorating the 10th-century ruler, Hywel ap Cadell, 'Hywel the Good', who convened a meeting of Welsh nobles here to codify the varied laws of the country. The remains of Whitland abbey are trifling, but deserve a brief mention. This was one of the greatest Cistercian establishments in Wales, the mother house to three other abbeys (including Strata Florida and Cwmhir), and was founded at the instigation of Bernard, the first Norman Bishop of St David's, in c. 1140. A colony of monks from Clairvaux initially settled at Treff-garne, before moving to the present site, a remote river valley 1¼ miles north of the present town, in 1151. Excavations by the Carmarthenshire Antiquarian Society in 1926 uncovered the foundations of the large cruciform church, and part of the adjacent cloister range. All that now survives are fragments of walls partly incorporated into modern boundaries, and extensive earthworks of the abbey and nearby fishponds.

CANNA'S WELL, LLANGAN (32)

Llangan West church is a remote, neglected building at the end of a lane off the Henllan Amgoed road, 2½ miles north-west of Whitland. According to legend, work on the original church was started in another part of the parish, but every night the stones and building materials were mysteriously transported to the present site, with a voice proclaiming *'Llangan, dyma'r fan'* ('Llangan, here is the place'). Curiously enough, the spot chosen lies within the ploughed-out site of an Iron Age hillfort, which was only discovered recently by aerial photography. Could the folk-tale be a garbled version of what occurred centuries ago, when the Early Christians decided to build a church within the hillfort to 'cleanse' a reputedly pagan area?

The existing parish church is Victorian in fabric, but Medieval in appearance, with a chancel, nave and north porch. In the field to the north-east is a marshy spring dedicated to St Canna, and formerly renowned for medicinal properties. The long, elaborate cure invovled contact with a nearby boulder called Canna's Chair, which is inscribed with the letters 'CANV'. After making an offering of pins, the patient would drink, or wash in the water, and then sit on the 'chair'. The healing powers were believed to increase if the patient managed to sleep on the rock, and the treatment continued for days, even up to a fortnight or more. Until the last century the well was frequently visited and hundreds of pins could be seen there; but when the landowner removed soil from around the spring, the waters failed and the site gradually became neglected and abandoned.

ST CLEARS (33)

St Clears is now a decayed market town neatly bisected by the A40, the southern half, or 'old town', representing the core of the Medieval settlement established by the Normans in the early 12th century.

The **parish church** of St Mary is set back from the road on the riverbank, and is reached along a tree-lined avenue. This was a Priory cell of the Cluniac Order — a monastic off shoot of the Benedictines — and a daughter-house of St 6Martin-de-champs, Paris. Like other 'alien' priories, St Clears had an unsettled existence during the frequent wars between England and France, and in

St. Clears; the priory church of St. Mary.

44

1414 it was dissolved by Henry V, and the property later granted to All Soul's College, Oxford. As the priory was served by no more than three monks, any conventional buildings would not have been of any great extent, and have, in any case, disappeared. The existing building is a typical Welsh parish church in scale and layout, and gives little indication of its monastic origin. The spacious, well-kept interior of this largely 13th-century church confuses the eye, for there appears to be no perpendicular lines; the walls lean outwards at precarious angles, and even the splendid late Norman chancel arch is lop-sided. This arch is undoubtedly the most impressive surviving feature of the church. The decorated capitals and columns are cross-hatched with chisel marks, carved into the cold stone by an unknown mason 800 years ago.

The second survivor of the Medieval settlement is a **motte and bailey castle** a short distance to the south. The large oval bailey is ignominiously used as a recreation park, and children now play where the timber buildings of the ruthless Norman lords once stood. When Gerald of Wales and Archbishop Baldwin passed through this district on a preaching tour in 1188 a violent, but not uncommon, act drew the attention of the travellers. A young Welshman on his way to meet the party was murdered by a group of archers from the castle. Baldwin 'turned aside from the road, ordered the bloody corpse to be wrapped in his almoner's cloak, and with pious supplication commended the soul of the murdered youth to heaven'. The following day the soldiers were conscripted into the army Baldwin was gathering for the Crusades, as a punishment for the crime. The castle had been in existence long before that event and, despite its occasional capture and destruction by the Welsh, remained in use well into the 15th century. It is possible that the timber keep on the motte was replaced with a stone tower, but only grass-grown earthworks remain today.

LAUGHARNE (34)

Laugharne is rapidly becoming a shrine for Dylan Thomas pilgrims, but this town on the muddy estuary of the Taf has much to offer the visiting antiquarian and sightseer. Laugharne was founded by the Normans in the late 11th or early 12th century on a ridge above the confluence of the rivers Corran and Taf, hence the original Welsh name, *Abercorran*. It was one of three great fortresses designed to guard the adjacent estuaries of the Taf, Tywi and Gwendraeth (see also Llansteffan and Kidwelly), and indicates the importance attached to water-borne communications by the invaders.

In 1172 Henry II stopped at Laugharne on his way back from Ireland, and met with the Welsh ruler, Lord Rhys. By this time in Henry's turbulent career, the king was in need of all the friends and supporters he could get, and so was willing to come to some arrangement with the powerful Welshman. On Henry's death in 1189 Rhys rebelled against the new authority, and the castles of Llansteffan and Laugharne were his first victims. Both were regained by the English, but fell again to the Welsh in 1215 and 1257.

Some years after the last attack, a major rebuilding programme was initiated by the Lord of Laugharne, Sir Guy de Brian. Only two large round towers and part of the outer gatehouse survives of this work; one of the towers is intact up to battlement level, and is roofed over with a pointed stone dome. A further, and more substantial, rebuilding took place in the late 16th century when the old fortress was purchased by the flamboyant Sir John Perrot, about whom we shall be hearing more later on. Perrot adapted and transformed the late 13th-century castle into a palatial residence, with internal ranges of half-timbered buildings, a multi-windowed entrance porch and a formal garden with an ornamental fountain. After Sir John's death the building suffered through the neglect and indifference of successive tenant owners (one is reputed to have burnt down the hall to disguise the fact that he had stolen the lead from the roof). During the Civil War Laugharne was garrisoned for the king, but when the Roundhead army started bombarding the castle, the garrison wisely surrendered. The castle's descent into an overgrown and dangerous ruin has been halted by CADW: Welsh Historic Monuments, and the surviving masonry is being consolidated prior to opening.

Beyond the castle gates a settlement grew up, which may have been protected by a timber palisade and stone gateways. Nothing now survives of these defences, and the actual area enclosed is believed to have been very small when compared with the other fortified towns in west Wales. A number of fine Georgian houses remain, but the

Laugharne; the castle seen from the foreshore.

earliest domestic building is the 17th-century Island House below the castle.

Laugharne church. Further along the St Clears road stands the secluded 15th-century parish church of St Martin. The exterior of this large, cruciform building is suitably impressive, but the interior is overwhelming. The plain, unwhitewashed walls are encrusted with a great number of mural tablets commemorating various noteables including, of course, Dylan Thomas, who is buried in the south churchyard.

> 'Mortality behold and fear
> What a change of flesh is here'

is one stern 18th century warning confronting the visitor. A pair of grinning, winged Death's heads

on another plaque is in a similar vein. The roofs are modern, and the line of the steeply-pitched Medieval roofs are visible at a lower level on the tower walls. The unadorned and rugged stonework of the lofty crossing arches gives an impression of austerity and great strength. In the north transept is a canopied niche containing a female effigy, while in the opposite transept is a diminutive Celtic cross of 9th or 10th-century date. This cross was found in the churchyard, and suggests that the church was a pre-Norman foundation. One last little treasure deserves to be singled out; at the top of the easternmost window of the nave is a collection of 14th-century stained glass — a rare survival — bearing the arms of Sir Guy de Brian and the crowned head of Edward III.

COYGEN HILLFORT (35)

Leaving Laugharne along the A4066 road to Pendine, the visitor passes several archaeological sites of note. At the hilltop village of Broadway can be seen the solitary surviving wall of **Roche Castle**, a Medieval moated site with the ivy-covered remains of a first-floor hall. This belonged to the De La Rupe family (from whence the name derives) and was held briefly by Sir John Perrot in the 16th century. The countryside immediately west of Roche is still marked by the long, narrow, unenclosed fields of Medieval origin — a rare surviving example of early agricultural practices.

Continuing along towards Pendine the road passes the site of Coygen cave and hillfort, recently reduced to a pile of rubble through quarrying for limestone. The cave was known to antiquarians as far back as c. 1800 when a remarkable Romano-British bronze incense shaker was discovered in the vicinity. Fenton explored 'some very lofty and curius natural chambers in the limestone rock', and

Coygen cave; excavations in progress c. 1913. (Copyright: Carmarthen Museum).

a later 19th-century visitor found the cave floor 'strewn with the bones of extinct mammalia'.

The first major excavation was in 1913, when Herbert Eccles removed over 150 tons of debris and unearthed another of the cave's many entrances (see photograph). Relics of early man were confined to a few flint chips, but the plentiful remains of Ice Age animals included Mammoth, Elk, Reindeer and Wolf. The excavation halted abruptly in August 1914, and Eccles wrote: 'our eyes were turned to face a greater beast than ever terrorised primeval man — a beast endowed with all the powers of human thought'; and so Kaiser Wilhelm brought the Coygen dig to a close. Further work in 1933 and 1963 produced more remains of extinct animals, and two stone hand axes, shaped by Neanderthal Man around 60,000 years ago.

Excavations at the hillfort revealed that the summit of Coygen rock was occupied in the Mesolithic, Neolithic, and late Bronze Age/early Iron Age periods. Then in the 2nd century BC, a group of continental immigrants settled here, and fortified their hilltop farmstead with a rubble bank and rock-cut ditch. This fort appears to have been abandoned in the Roman period, and the defences were ruinous when, in the years 270-300 AD, a renewed and intensive period of occupation occurred. A great number of finds included imported 'samian' ware, bronze and metal implements (some brought to the camp as scrap to be reworked), glass beads and plenty of animal bones, indicating the importance of stock-rearing at that time. However, the inhabitants of the fort were also engaged on a more lucrative venture, for beside one of the huts a concealed hoard of forged Roman coins was discovered! The tantalizing discovery of a few fragments of imported earthenware vessels of 5th-7th century date, suggests that the derelict hillfort was reoccupied for a time in the Dark Ages.

LLANDAWKE (36)

This tiny 14th-century church lies hidden away in the wooded vales 1½ miles west of Laugharne, and can hardly be described as one of the most frequented religious buildings in this part of Wales. The whole church exudes an aura of gentle decay. In summer the churchyard is a waist-high jungle of nettles and cow-parsley, and green leaves fringe the Victorian stained-glass windows. Llandawke is

Llandawke; the parish church.

a small and unsophisticated building with a whitewashed chancel, nave and a stumpy west tower. From the vaulted ground floor of the tower a tiny door leads to a tortuously narrow stair winding up to the bell chamber, where a small window offers a view into the nave. In the chancel there is a sedilia with knight's heads on the canopy, and also a broken female effigy, perhaps that of Margaret Marloes, daughter of Guy de Brian. Beside the chancel arch is a 5th-early 6th-century inscribed slab commemorating *Barrivendus, son of Vendubarus*; a '*hic iacit*' is scrawled on one side of the slab, as if an afterthought. An Ogham inscription along the edge commemorates another Dark Age worthy, one *Dumeledonas*, and was probably added at a slightly later date by a parsimonious Irish stone carver. Another inscribed stone of similar age can be found at the nearby of Llansadurnen, half a mile south of Llandawke, just off the Pendine-Laugharne road. This large stone carries a 6th-century Latin inscription in memory of *Totavalus, son of Dothorantus*, and is kept inside the 19th-century parish church.

PARC Y GERRIG SANCTAIDD (37)

The Laugharne and Pendine area of west Wales is particularly rich in stone memorials of the Dark Ages. Their presence at Llandawke (36), Laugharne (34), Llansadurnen and Eglwys Cymmin (39) indicates a pre-Norman origin for these Medieval buildings, but the remarkable and little-known Parc y Gerrig Sanctaidd ('Field of the holy stones') is an Early Christian site which did not evolve into a later church.

All that remains today is a stone wall surrounding a dence thicket in a field beside the Llansadurnen-Eglwys Cymmin road. Within the enclosure, and half hidden by the undergrowth, are two stones, one carved with a simple ring-cross of 7th-9th century type, and the other with a hollowed-out depression on its upper surface. According to local tradition, pins were dipped into the water-filled hollow and then used to prick warts, in the belief that this would lead to a cure. Present-day sufferers are not recommended to try this unhygenic method. It was also a custom for funeral corteges passing this way to rest the coffin on the stones for a while. When the site was excavated in 1889 and 1901, the remains of a drystone enclosure, measuring 8½ × 7feet, was uncovered. This may

well have been the foundations of an early church contemporary with the ring-cross. A modern wall now marks the site of the enclosure.

CWMBRWYN (38)

Only low earthworks survive above ground today at Cwmbrwyn, but excavations in 1905-6 uncovered the remains of substantial fortified farmstead of the 2nd-4th centuries AD. The site lies about 2 miles north-east of Eglwys Cymmin, alongside a minor road to New Mill, and is mis-leading marked on OS maps as a 'Roman fortlet'. The defences comprised an earthen rampart with an outer, 9 foot deep ditch. The bank may have been topped with a palisade, or an equally formid-able thorn hedge.

This was a native equivalent of a Roman villa, a farmstead modelled along the lines of the 'civilized' country houses built by the invaders elsewhere in lowland Wales. Gone were the dingy, draughty, thatched round huts of the Iron Age; the well-to-do owners of Cwmbrwyn resided in a stone and timber house with glazed windows and a slate roof. There was probably underfloor heating to take the bite off the Welsh weather, and, luxury of luxuries, a heated indoor bath suite. There were querns for hand grinding corn, spindleworls for weaving, and imported *amphorae* storage jars for wine or other consumables. The remainder of the courtyard was taken up by less substantial buildings including a forge and smithy. A gravelled road approached the stone gateway on the east side. All is now a vague earthwork on the edge of a cornfield.

EGLWYS CYMMYN (39)

This is a remarkable and atmospheric site, seemingly lost in the backlanes of the rolling countryside of west Carmarthenshire. The church lies roughly half-way between Red Roses and Pendine, beside the B4314, and the building is ringed with the earthworks of what may have been an Iron Age fort, or an even earlier 'pagan' ritual site. Slighter earthworks also indicate the remains of a deserted Medieval village in the fields west and east of the church.

St Margaret's church is a simple and austere 14th-century building, believed to have been the work of Margaret Marloes, daughter of the Lord of Laugharne. Both nave and chancel are roofed over with pointed stone vaults (the chancel was rebuilt in 1877-8), and the ghost-like remains of paintings and biblical texts of 16th-18th century date adorn the walls. In the nave is a 5th-early 6th century inscribed stone commemorating *Avittoria, daughter of Cunignus*. The inscription is in Latin and Ogham, indicating that the two languages were in use in this area 1500 years ago. Cunignus is also named on one of the Llanfihangel Croesfeini stones (21), and he may be identified as St Cynin, one of the sons of King Brychan of Brecon.

MORFA BYCHAN TOMBS (40)

These four megalithic burial chambers lie on a boulder-strewn hillside overlooking Morfa Bychan bay, just under a mile west of the holiday resort at Pendine. A footpath has recently been cleared up to the chambers, which lie below an outcrop of millstone grit near the top. The best preserved tomb lies north of the 'Druid's Altar' (a natural rock pillar), the 9½ feet capstone covers a rectangular chamber which was formed by digging a hollow under the stone, and propping it up with slabs. An entrance passage led into the chamber from the north side. The other tombs are more ruined, but two still retain traces of a surrounding cairn mound. The tombs appear to have been robbed of their contents at an early date, for only bits of charcoal and flint flakes were found during excavations in 1910.

Further north along the ridge are numerous remains of a deserted settlement of Medieval origin; field walls, enclosures, agricultural 'clearance cairns' and house sites. On the opposite side of Morfa Bychan is a small promontory fort beside the cliff path to Pendine. In front of the main rampart with its rock-cut ditch can be seen a stone enclosure or pound, once believed to have been a ritual circle.

MARROS (41)

A mile or so west of Pendine, beside the Amroth road, stands the impressive hilltop church of Marros, rebuilt in the last century except for the sturdy Medieval tower. An unusual war memorial on the green, in the form of a Stonehenge 'trillithon', is said to incorporate genuine Bronze Age standing stones brought from elsewhere in the parish. Top Castle on the cliffs one mile south-west of the church is a univallate Iron Age enclosure

almost encircled by modern quarries, and reached by a steep path from the beach.

Further west at Trelissey is another hilltop stronghold. Excavations in 1950-1 uncovered the foundations of a stone building within the interior of this 340 foot diameter enclosure. Some potsherds of Medieval date were found, but the main period of occupation was between the early second, and the late third century AD. The presence of some pieces of coal and iron slag suggests that the Romano-British occupants carried out metal-working, and the site is comparable to the fortified farmstead at nearby Cwmbrwyn(38).

AMROTH (42)

Leaving the old county of Carmarthenshire, we now enter Pembrokeshire. The Medieval parish church of Amroth lies on the hillside above the modern seaside hamlet which bears its name. Fenton described the church as 'a singular little building with its tower oddly disposed of', a reference to the position of the battlemented tower on the north side of the nave, rather than the more usual west side. The rest of the building consists of a chancel, north aisle and south transept, all thoroughly restored in 1899. An eroded mound beside the church is all that remains of an earth and timber motte castle set up by the Norman lord of the district.

LUDCHURCH (43)

Quarrying for limestone in the 18th century has left this Medieval church standing high and dry on a rocky 'island' in the middle of the flooded workings. The church lies beside a minor road from Narberth to Amroth, and is approached along a remaining causeway of rock. The building is mainly of 13th and 14th century date, a simple chancel and nave, to which was added a south aisle and tower in the 15th century. Beside the door is a holy water stoup carved with a human head; more pagan-looking heads adorn the capitals of the aisle arcade.

About a mile north-east of Ludchurch is a group of Bronze Age burial mounds in a field on the left of the Tavernspite road. Further along the same ridge is a more important mound, **Crug Swllt (44)**, on the outskirts of the village. This barrow found a new lease of life in the 18th century when it was used as a base for a gallows. The site was excavated in the early 19th century by Richard Fenton, in his usual haphazard fashion. Fenton employed local workmen to dig into the mound, although he himself lent a helping hand, and brought his pick-axe crashing down onto a delicate Bronze Age urn. This was evidently a secondary burial, for the central cist was soon reached, which contained some charcoal and burnt bones. Unfortunately for Fenton, the labourers soon gave up digging, after finding no 'treasure', and running out of ale!

The antiquarian also recorded an earthwork enclosure with a recumbent stone inside, in a field south-west of the barrow. The enclosure was approached by a raised causeway, and the whole site seems to have been a Prehistoric 'henge', or ritual enclosure. Sadly, nothing survives of this today.

BEGELLY (45)

This is the most accessible of several tall-towered Medieval parish churches in the vicinity. The others worth visiting are: Jeffreyston, a 13th-14th century building with an unusual triple-gabled south facade; Reynalton, an undivided chancel and nave with a 16th-century transept and tower; and Loveston, an imposing, if somewhat neglected 15th-16th century cruciform building with a domed roof to the tower, and vaulted transepts. The latter two churches beckon to each other across the wooded Cresswell valley. The 'ton' element in the place-name refers to the settlements which grew up around the churches, but only that at Jeffreyston is more than a cluster of farmhouses.

Back to Begelly, the most familiar and, as previously mentioned, the most accessible of these buildings. It lies on a low hill just north of the Tenby-Narberth roundabout on the A478. The church was restored in 1886 and consists of the usual chancel and nave, with later additions including a north aisle, south transept and battlemented tower. An 18th-century bell in the tower was cast by Bayley of Bridgewater: 'My sound is good, my shape is neat, Twas Bayley made me so complete' runs the verse on the side of the bell. Below the church stood an earthwork castle of the Norman lord of the manor of Begelly. Only a few irregular mounds can be seen today, for the castle was apparently destroyed to make way for a graveyard extension.

CRESSWELL CASTLE (46)

Cresswell Quay is a delightful place to visit in summer, a winding tree-cloaked valley on the upper reaches of the Cleddau, with a cluster of houses and cottages grouped around an old stone quay, from where locally-mined anthracite coal used to be exported. Across the river on the heavily afforested west bank, can just be glimpsed the ivy-covered walls of the 'Castle', one of the lesser-known examples of upper class domestic architecture in west Wales. It is believed to have been built by William Barlow, Bishop of St David's (1536-48), and the few identifiable details accord well with a 16th-century date. The property later passed to William's brother. Roger Barlow of Slebech, and it continued to be occupied into the 17th century. The remains comprise an oblong enclosure with four corner towers, one of which is a dovecote. Buildings were ranged against the inner walls, and a detached three-storey block occupied the open side facing the river.

Nearby are the ruins of a building, believed to have been a chapel, and a holywell, Christ's Well, hence the place-name. Whether this was an earlier ecclesiastical establishment, or the private chapel of the Elizabethan owners of the Castle, is unclear. This uncertainty existed as far back as the 16th century when the property was described as 'a certen chapell or tenemente called Creswells'; and Fenton who evidently did not visit the remains, made an off-hand reference to 'a chapel called Christ's Well'.

As a castle, Cresswell is a miserable failure, for not only is the building in a very vulnerable position, overlooked by high ground, but the walls are thin and the towers too small and ineffective to offer much resistance. In fact, Cresswell is a mansion dressed up as a Medieval stronghold by a rich landowner, who chose to build in the style of his feudal forebears.

MINWEAR (47)

This secluded, tree-ringed church lies 2½ miles south-west of Canaston Bridge, at the end of a wooded lane off the Martletwy road. The manor of Minwear was granted in 1150 to the Order of the Knights Hospitallers, whose Commandery lay across the river at Slebech (53). The original 12th-century church was probably a simple oblong building (the present nave) with a round headed

Cresswell Castle; a suggested reconstruction of the 16th century house.

doorway in the south wall. When the chancel was added later, the east wall of the nave was pierced with a series of low arches, and two small 'windows' cut through the wall higher up. This is in complete contrast to the more usual large and spacious chancel arches found in other churches. A south transept, north aisle and bell turret were added in the 15th-16th century. The Norman font has four heads carved on the side, probably representing the four evangelists, but years of ignominious use as a horse trough has taken its toll.

Beyond the church a public footpath leads down to the banks of the Eastern Cleddau where, in a dense wood on the left, can be found the extensive and puzzling remains of the 'Sister's House'. A broad road leads past ruined and overgrown enclosure walls, barns, cartsheds and dwellings. There are the remains of at least two vaulted

buildings, and several miniature 'tower houses' of a type similar to others in west Wales (see 91, 106). The most impressive building is the shell of a huge, 16th-century tithe barn, over 100 feet long. This complex has been variously interpreted as a monastic site, a grange or hostel, belonging to the nearby Commandery. Fenton was probably nearer the mark when he described the site as a *'considerable ruin of a respectable mansion'*, and the 'sister' element of the place-name may be due to a misreading of 'Systerne House' (so named in a grant of 1546), a possible reference to the adjacent well and fishpond.

TEMPLETON (48)

The 'Temple' element in the place-name gives the game away, for this village owes it origins to the Knights Templar, the powerful military brethren formed to protect pilgrims on the hazardous route to Jerusalem. It is not known for certain what the warrior-monks established here — a church or hospice perhaps — but nothing now survives except the modern church of St John. Under the patronage and protection of the Templars a village grew up which, even today, retains the layout and extent of its Medieval forerunner. The single street was lined with houses which had narrow burgage plots running behind them. These plots have been 'fossilized' by later field walls and hedges.

Just west of the village stands the tree-covered remains of Sentance Castle, a Norman ringwork which may have been built to defend the adjoining settlement. The villagers received their water supply from St Margaret's holy well in a field north of the castle. This fresh, cool spring has been enclosed with a protective shell of masonry with a modern slate roof.

'The cottages in this village have an appearance of great antiquity, and the remains of numerous

Templeton; old house with a lateral chimney.

ruined buildings . . . afford evidence of it having been at one time a place of greater importance' wrote the topographer Samuel Lewis c. 1833. No ruined buildings are visible today, but two of the 'cottages' have prominent lateral projecting chimneys, indicating a late Medieval origin. The Poyer's Arms (dated 1672) was formerly renowned for home-made *Kitcats*, or *Cat's Pies* — but animal lovers take comfort, this was merely another name for mutton pies!

NARBERTH (49)

Virtually every guidebook which includes an entry on this market town invariably mentions Narberth's part in the Welsh folk-tales, 'The Mabinogion'. Although these tales were written down in the 14th century, they embody centuries of oral storytelling, and name Narberth as the chief court of Pwyll, Lord of the seven cantrefs of Dyfed. This legendary origin has little bearing on the development of the historic town, and indeed, the 'Arberth' of the Mabinogion may not be in Pembrokeshire at all, but north-east of Cardigan where there is a river Arberth at the foot of a strange, isolated hill (perhaps the magical 'gorsedd' of the tales). It is not known for certain when the Normans established the present castle and town; it is generally believed that Sentance Castle at Templeton (48) was the original stronghold here, but there seems to be no good reason for accepting this, and the existing stone castle may well occupy the site of the 12th-century Norman earthwork. A 'castle in Arberth' (the name of the surrounding district) was captured and damaged by the Welsh in 1116, 1215 and 1257, and it was after the last attack that much of the existing stonework was added. The castle passed to Sir Rhys ap Thomas in the 15th century, and following the death of his grandson the property was confiscated by the Crown and surveyed. This valuable survey gives a detailed description of the layout and buildings within the castle. There were five towers, a great hall, kitchen, a gallery and a 'great chamber', plus a twin-towered gatehouse which has entirely vanished. At the highest part of the site (on the earlier motte?) stood a four-storey keep with a dungeon at the lowest level. Today little remains apart from two corner towers and a fragment of the keep and hall.

The Medieval town lay outside the castle gates to the north and west, and may have been enclosed

Narberth; one of the ruined towers of the castle.

with timber palisades and stone gateways. No evidence for these defences now survives, but a rectangular gatehouse is shown on an 18th-century engraving of Narberth, which appears to have formed part of the town walls rather than the castle. St Andrew's church was rebuilt in 1879, but the adjacent Plas Farm is the only obvious early building surviving in the town, with a prominent corbelled chimney and a filled-in mullioned window suggesting a 16th-century date.

CAERAU AND LLANDDEWI GAER (50)

Two fine examples of Iron Age defended settlements, lying only a quarter of a mile apart on a ridge above Lampeter Vale, Narberth. Both are on private land, but the earthworks are visible from nearby roads, and a public footpath runs past Caerau. This is a univallate enclosure, 300 feet across, with an encircling ditch and 10 feet high rampart. Remains of a possible outer enclosure survive on the north-east side. A Neolithic stone

axe was found here in 1816, but the site is undoubtedly of Iron Age date.

The nearby Llanddewi Gaer lies a short distance further east, on the hilltop above Llanddewi Efelfre church. It is a multivallate promontory fort, with three powerful lines of defence guarding the west and north sides. The entrance is at the east termination of the grass-grown ramparts.

ROBESTON WATHEN (51)

The hilltop church of Robeston Wathen is a tasteful Victorian rebuilding of the Medieval structure, but is nevertheless an impressive building in an impressive location, and worth a brief visit by travellers hurrying along the A40 to Haverfordwest. Just beyond the village, on the right-hand side of the road, is a small enclosure of probable Iron Age date. This is a classic example of a 'hillslope site', with a single crescentic rampart and ditch defending the settlement on the vulnerable uphill side.

LLAWHADEN (52)

Llawhaden today is a straggling village on a hill above the east branch of the river Cleddau, but it was formerly one of the most important boroughs under the control of the Bishops of St David's. This one-time importance is attested by the large and imposing shell of the Bishop's Castle at the east end of the village, and also by the less obvious remains of a 'hospital' and the large parish church of St Aidan. The origin of the settlement is not clear. There was a castle here by 1175, when it was visited by Gerald of Wales. The Bishop's dwelling lay within a circular palisaded enclosure, surrounded by a deep ditch (a formidable object to cross even today), but the timber buildings were razed by the Welsh in 1192. Masonry defences were erected in the following century, but the whole castle was remodelled by Bishop Martyn and his successors in the late 13th-early 14th century, obscuring the line of the earlier defences. Martyn added a U-shaped residential block on one side of the Norman ringwork, with a chapel, bakehouse, and guest chambers ranged against the inner curtain wall. There was also a mess hall for the Bishop's private army. The last major addition to the castle was a twin-towered facade to the gatehouse, which still stands to full height, although the rest of the gatehouse has fallen.

The rebuilding of the castle was probably the impetus for the development of the adjacent town. In 1287 Bishop Bek founded a hospital to care for poor wayfarers and the elderly and infirm. Since this establishment also functioned as a leper house, it was set beyond the limits of the borough. Today only the chapel remains, a simple, one-roomed building with a high vaulted roof. The old parish church appears to have been rebuilt at this time, and during further work in the 15th century part of the earlier building was incorporated into the new; the outlines of the tower, for instance, can be seen embedded within its larger successor. A 10th-century ring-cross has been set into the chancel wall.

Llawhaden Castle from a 19th century etching.

SLEBECH OLD CHURCH (53)

We have the first Baron de Runtzen of Slebech Hall to thank for the present condition of the Medieval parish church — a roofless, crumbling shell on the banks of the Cleddau. In summer this atmospheric ruin is almost engulfed in undergrowth, although the interior is clear, and the tall, thin tower rises from the surrounding jungle like a beacon. In 1838 the Baron built a new church (aptly described as *'be-spired, but uninspiring'*) in a more accessible part of the parish. This building contains two alabaster effigies brought from the old church, which was allowed to decay. Slebech old church can be reached by a public footpath from Blackpool Mill or Picton Castle (a long walk either way), and lies in the grounds of a gloomy mansion, built on the site of the Commandery of the Knights Hospitallers. Like the Templars, this organization was formed to protect pilgrims on the Jerusalem road, and owned extensive properties in Britain. They inherited the Templar estates when that order was suppressed in the 14th century.

Most of the existing cruciform church is of 15th-early 16th century date, with some later additions belonging to the post-Reformation period, when the estate was purchased by the Barlow family. Sir William Hamilton lies buried here with his first wife (whom he despised), rather than with his second wife, the notorious Lady Emma, Nelson's paramour. Fenton's description of the church provides us with a glimpse of the building before its dismantling: 'the floor of the nave is paved with small painted bricks [ie. tiles] . . . and that of the chancel with black and white marble. The roof of the latter is ceiled with wood in square compartments, with a flower in each angle, and overlaid with the Barlow arms'. The roof is now open to the sky, and weeds and grass carpet the interior.

PICTON CASTLE (54)

Mighty Picton Castle has been mellowed over the centuries and reduced to the status of a 'stately home', although it is unfortunately not open to the public. The exterior can, however, be viewed by visitors on their way to the Graham Sutherland art gallery in the remodelled stable block. The castle lies near the junction of the two Cleddau rivers, about 3½ miles south-east of Haverfordwest, and the gallery is usually open April to September.

Slebech; inside the ruined parish church.

Picton Castle was built at the end of the 13th century, possibly by Sir John Wogan, Justiciary of Ireland, to replace either a nearby earthwork, or the archaic motte and bailey at Wiston (55). It was built to a plan typical of the time; a rectangular enclosure with round towers at the angles, and a twin-towered gatehouse. There may have been a fifth tower on the west side, later replaced by an incongruous castellated block by Lord Milford in the 18th century. Extensive modern alterations have softened the war-like features of the building, and Fenton's detailed description of Picton is that of a Georgian country house, rather than a grim, Medieval stronghold.

During the Civil War Picton Castle was garrisoned for the King by Sir Richard Philipps. The story goes that the castle was surrendered when Philipps' infant son was kidnapped from his nursemaid's arms, when she leant out of the nursery window to receive a letter from a Roundhead soldier.

WISTON CASTLE (55)

Three miles to the north of Picton is an older, and far less modernized stronghold. Wiston was probably founded in the early 12th century by a Flemish immigrant named Wizo (hence the name 'Wizo's town' = Wiston). To defend his hold on the land, this entrepreneur built a very large and strong motte and bailey castle on the broad summit of a hill. Indeed, it was so powerful that the Welsh only managed to capture it 'with great toil and conflict' in 1147. The Chronicles also inform us that Wiston was captured 'by treachery' in 1193, when its Lord, Philip fitz Wizo, and his family were taken prisoner by the Welsh. After another devastating raid in 1220 the castle is mentioned no more, and it may be assumed that it was never rebuilt. Only extensive earthworks and a ruined shell-keep on the motte now survive. The keep was entered through a round-headed doorway in the south wall, and there was probably timber lean-to buildings ranged against the inner wall. Accommodation must have been very cramped, and the main domestic buildings were undoubtedly situated in the bailey.

A small town was also established here in the 12th century, and it is not unreasonable to suppose that this settlement was initially sheltered within the abnormally large bailey. The adjacent manor house is said to incorporate remains of the Medieval residence of the influential Wogan family (effigies believed to be that of Sir Henry

Wogan and his wife can be seen at Slebech church). The parish church of St Mary lies to the south of the castle, and was extensively restored in 1866. The 14th-century nave is believed to be the oldest part of the building, the chancel was rebuilt in the 16th century.

BOULSTON CHURCH AND OLD HALL (56)

There is surely no other church in west Wales which can lay claim to be so overgrown or neglected as Boulston. A veritable jungle of brambles and nettles engulf the roofless shell of this church, once of the private mausoleum of the Wogan family. Their great mansion lies equally overgrown a short distance downstream. Boulston was acquired by a branch of the Wogans of Picton in the 15th century, and the estate remained with the family until the late 18th century.

The church lies on the north bank of the Cleddau, where the tidal river sweeps around in a great curve past Boulston and Hook. A signposted public footpath leaves the Uzmaston road about 2½ miles south-east of Haverfordwest, and can be followed past the new Hall down to the river. The trees and bushes which obscure the church have even taken root inside; scattered about the chancel are fragments of dressed stones and broken memorial tablets, testifying to the long-departed glories of this Pembrokeshire family. One tumbled slab is richly carved with the crest and coat-of-arms of the Wogans. A tiny child effigy has been removed for safe-keeping to nearby Uzmaston church. This effigy is a survivor of the earlier Medieval church, for the existing building was constructed in the Gothic style around 1843.

Downstream, a gloomy forest marches to the water's edge, hiding the shattered remains of Boulston Old Hall. According to legend the surrounding countryside was terrorized by a fearsome basilisk, a dragon-like creature which could kill simply by gazing at its victim, but could itself be killed if it was seen first. A Wogan hid inside a barrel and, by staring out through the bung-hole, succeeded in destroying the basilisk before it could return the killing gaze. The location of the Old Hall is an apt place for people to have imagined the existence of such a creature. The site is low-lying and marshy, shrouded in trees, and here and there

Boulston; tumbled monuments in the ruined church.

ragged openings lead down into the dark cellar of the original Medieval hall. The walls are up to 6 feet thick, and it is tempting to think that this could, in fact, have been the tower of an earlier castle. In the 16th century two multi-storey towers were added at either end of the hall, and a series of walled courtyards and gardens built. This palatial residence was an imposing status-symbol and an obvious indication of Wogan wealth and prestige to any river-borne traveller, in the days when the Cleddau was a much frequented highway. The remains of the watergate can be seen — a large arch just above the high tide mark — where ships could unload their cargoes, and from where the lords of Boulston could embark on a pleasant evenings boat journey along the river.

All is now faded glory, and the crumbling walls alone remain. This tangible atmosphere of decay is not only confined to the house and church; the new Hall is looking run-down, and there are derelict farms and houses adjoining the little-frequented road. Visitors passing through the woods are now likely to be startled only by the whirring flight of an occasional pheasant, rather than meeting a beady-eyed basilisk.

Nevern, Newport and the Preseli Mountains

(Sites 57–87)

CLYDAI CHURCH (57)

Clydai lies in a remote valley near the boundary between the old counties of Carmarthenshire and Pembrokeshire. The nearest large village is Boncath, about three miles to the north-west, although an easier route to Clydai is via the Crymmyrch to Bwlch-y-Groes road. The church itself is a typical Medieval building with a chancel, nave and west tower (all thoroughly restored in the last century), but it also contains a collection of three Dark Age stones. Two carry bilingual Latin and Ogham inscriptions in memory of 'Etternus, son of Victor' and 'Dovatucis'; the latter stone has an additional Maltese cross of 7th-9th century date. The third stone has a Latin inscription only, 'Solini filius vendoni' = Solinus, son of Vendonius.

FRENNI-FAWR (58)

Three miles due west of Clydai is Frenni-fawr, an outlier of the Preseli Mountains. In legend the summit was used as a campsite by the Roman Emperor Maxen, but in reality this isolated height was a burial ground for the élite of the local Bronze Age tribes. The mountain can be reached from either the Crymmyrch road or the A478. A total of five cairns survive, the best preserved rising 5 feet high. At the beginning of the 19th century Richard Fenton excavated several of the mounds in the space of a few hours. The first contained a burial cist and urn, but two others (which Fenton excavated simultaneously) had been previously despoiled and only a ruined cist was found.

BAYVIL GAER (59)

Many churches in West Wales are known to occupy the site of Early Christian graveyards, but the earthwork known as Y Gaer is a Dark Age cemetery which never received a later church. The site lies beside a minor road from the B4582 to Moylgrove, two miles north-east of Nevern (61), and consists of an eroded oval enclosure of probable Iron Age date. Stone-lined graves were discovered inside the enclosure in the 1920s, and a trial excavation by the Dyfed Archaeological

Trust in 1979 indicated that the interior is tightly packed with burials. Fragments of human bones from one of the graves were radio-carbon dated to the late 7th-early 8th century AD. This was evidently an important local Christian cemetery, but what is less clear is whether this represents a change in use of an occupied hillfort, or whether this was a derelict site taken over and reused by the Early Christians.

CASTELL HENLLYS (60)

Just under two miles south of Y Gaer is another Iron Age hillfort which found a new use centuries after it was built. Here at Castell Henllys, the fort has been used, not as a graveyard, but as an example of 'experimental archaeology' in re-creating life in the Iron Age.

The hillfort lies just off the A487 near Eglwyswrw, and occupies a promontory site above a tributary valley of the Nevern river. The settlement was defended by a strong bank, ditch and counterscarp on the north side, with the remainder of the enclosure protected by an additional bank and the steep natural slopes. There was an additional embanked enclosure (or Romano-British date) guarding the main approach. Excavations in 1980-86 revealed that the north rampart overlaid an earlier *chevaux-de-frise* — a rare defensive feature consisting of a row of upright stones designed to counter any chariot-borne attack. The inner rampart had three constructional phases: an original clay rubble bank, then an additional layer of pebbles and a timber palisade, finally modified with shale revetments and a new stockade. The uniqueness of Castell Henllys is that recent work has not only been confined to excavation, for two of the round houses have been reconstructed, and during the summer months imaginative activities (such as woad growing, Celtic feasts, Iron Age cuisine and metal-working) take place at this 2000-year-old, reborn, fort.

NEVERN (61)

A gloomy avenue of ancient yews leads the visitor up to the door of the parish church of Nevern, a place redolent with the spirit of antiquity. A church was founded here over 14 centuries ago by the Irish St Brynach, and a rich crop of legends, inscribed stones and Celtic crosses remain to indicate the importance attached to Nevern by Early Christians and Medieval pilgrims.

The existing cruciform building is probably of 13th-14th century date, with a sturdy 15th-century tower at the west end, but relics of its Dark Age precursor are never far away. Set into the window sills of the south chapel are two carved stones, one a 5th-early 6th-century Ogham and Latin memorial slab to Maglocunus, son of Clutorius. Lutorius, or Clethyr, is said to have been a local chieftan and Brychan's father-in-law (remember that marriages were permitted among the clergy of the Celtic church). Another bi-lingual stone of similar age stands in the churchyard next to the porch. The ragged Latin inscription commemorates Vitalianus, with an additional word, 'Emereto', which means either 'finished his work' or 'served with honour'. This has led to the suggestion that Vitalianus was a retired Roman soldier, but it could equally mean that he had finished his temporal service to God.

By far the most important of the Nevern stones is the great cross of St Brynach, a 12 feet high monument enriched with decorative panels of plait, key and knot-work. Along with the Carew Cross (99) this is one of the finest examples of Cel-

tic stone carving in Britain. The monument was set up around 1000 AD and so has nothing to do with the 6th-century saint.

One of the churchyard trees is known as the 'bleeding yew', from a dripping gash on the turnk which, according to legend, will only heal when a Welshman once more occupies the nearby castle. The most endearing of the many stories connected with this hallowed place, tells of a cuckoo which gave the first call of spring on St Brynach's Day (April 7th), while perched atop the cross. The story was known to the Pembrokeshire historian, George Owen (d. 1613, and who lies within the church), who wrote that the bird was so well-timed that the priest would wait for its call before celebrating Mass. One year the cuckoo was late. The congregation waited, and waited, and the priest began to despair of ever starting the service. But suddenly the bedraggled bird fluttered to rest on the cross, sang one note, and dropped dead. 'This vulgar tale', says Owen,' although it concerns in some sort church matters, you may either believe or not without peril of damnation'.

One more monument needs to be singled out to highlight Nevern's rich ecclesiastical heritage, the

Nevern; the rock-cut pilgrim's cross and (right) the 11th century 'St. Brynach's cross'.

'Pilgrim's Cross', which lies beside a signposted path on the way to the castle. On a rock face above the path can be seen the weathered outline of a cross, with a series of hollows or 'kneeling places' in the shale outcrop beneath. This wayside shrine was evidently a favoured stopping place of pilgrims engaged on the long and arduous journey to St David's. The wooded hilltop above the little village is the site of Nevern castle, a less hallowed relic of the Middle Ages. It was founded in the early 12th century by Robert fitz Martin, and survived as the stronghold and administrative centre of the surrounding Norman lordship of Cemmaes until 1191. In that year the castle was captured by the Welsh under Lord Rhys, and partially rebuilt in stone. Thereafter the Normans chose Newport (65) as a new centre for the lordship. The castle (which is freely accessible) consists of a large motte and bailey which may incorporate the earthworks of an earlier Iron Age fort. The tree-covered motte has the foundations of a round tower on the summit, and at the far end of the bailey there is a masonry square keep and wall added by the Welsh after 1191.

PENTRE IFAN BURIAL CHAMBER (62)

Undoubtedly the finest and best known Prehistoric monument in west Wales, Pentre Ifan lies about four miles south-east of Newport beside a signposted road from Temple Bar to Brynberian. This was one of the first archaeological sites to be protected by the earliest Ancient Monuments Act of 1882; hardly surprising, since Pentre Ifan was considered to be one of the 'diverse wonders' of Pembrokeshire as early as 1603. In that year the historian George Owen published a valuable account of the tomb, and included a drawing that not only shows the site as it then appeared (with more stones than remain now), but which is considered to be the earliest illustration of such a monument in wales.

The burial chamber was known to Owen as 'Maen y Gromlech', and he described it as 'a huge and massive stone mounted on highe and sett on the toppes of 3 other highe stones, pitched upright in the grounde, yet farre passeth for biggnes and height . . . anye other that ever I sawe, saveing some in Stonehenge upon Salisurie plaine . . . .' the

Pentre Ifan; the Neolithic burial chamber.

tomb consists of three upright slabs supporting a 16 feet long capstone almost 8 feet above ground level. Betwen the two southern supporters is a third 'portal' slab, while curving away on either side of the chamber is a semi-circular facade of stones (although only two of the stones remain upright today). The latter feature appears to have been mistaken by some early topographers as part of a stone circle. The long covering mound of stones extended north from the chamber for about 90 feet but has been robbed of material. The front of the cairn projected beyond the portal forming a funnel-shaped entrance or forecourt.

Pentre Ifan, with its portal stones and facades, resembles other Neolithic tombs in the vicinity of the Irish Sea, and it is probable that the builders had been influenced by the burial customs of the northern Ireland tribes.

BEDD YR AFANC (63)

The name means 'the lake monster's grave', but excavation in 1936 unfortunately revealed no trace of a monster interred in this curious Neolithic tomb. However, 'afanc' can also mean dwarf or beaver, and such a creature was believed to cause flooding in rivers and lakes. The tomb lies in an expanse of peat bog and heathland on the north flank of the Preseli mountains, just under half a mile south-east of Brynberian. Unlike other burial chambers in this area, the numerous stones which form the chamber are unusually small, and form the sides of a long, narrow grave passage in the middle of an oval mound. None of the stones is today higher than 3 feet, and presumably the chamber was roofed over with large slabs. Nevertheless, the monument is more characteristic of Neolithic Ireland than Wales. No evidence of dating material came to light during the excavation, but some time in the late 17th century the tomb was raided by treasure hunters, and 'an earthen pot w'th ashes and bones almost burnt' was discovered.

TAFARN Y BWLCH (64)

About two miles to the south-west is a scattered group of Bronze Age standing stones at Tafarn y

Bedd yr Afanc; a line of stones marks the extent of the burial chamber.

Bwlch, on the B4329 Eglwyswrw to New Inn road. The most obvious is a 6 feet high monolith incorporated into the roadside embankment. At the Waun Mawn road junction a track on the west passes close to three more stones, and can be followed for 1½ miles to the Garreg Hir standing stone overlooking the Gwaun valley. On high ground just north of the junction, and also reached by a footpath from the road, is another megalith group. One stone remains upright today, flanked by two recumbent slabs, both over 10 feet long. The stumps of two more stones can be traced. All of these may have formed one side of what was once a very large and imposing stone circle.

NEWPORT (65)

The founding of the historic town of Newport was due to the Norman invasion in the late 11th century, but there was undoubtedly some form of settlement here in far earlier times. On the banks of the river Nevern, north of the present town, is a semi-circular bank and ditch earthwork, a defended settlement of possible Iron Age date. But millenia before the introduction of iron into Britain, Prehistoric immigrants landed here and followed the river's course upstream to trade, hunt for food, and build new settlements. Many of these early 'frontiersmen' came from Ireland, bringing with them new ideas and beliefs which are reflected in the surviving monuments of the district. The chambered tombs of the Nevern valley show characteristic Irish influence in their design; in the Dark Ages a further batch of travellers introduced the *Ogham* script into west Wales, and then, in the late 11th century, the Normans arrived and carved out for themselves the marcher lordship of Cemmaes. Their original stronghold was at Nevern (61), but around c. 1200 it was abandoned and replaced by a new castle and town at the river's mouth. That castle was a large and strong ringwork on a ridge between two streams. These parallel streams also served to delineate the early town, which extended from the castle and church down to the sea.

Despite two devastating Welsh raids in the 13th century, the town thrived as the port and centre of

Newport; the castle.

Newport; Coetan Arthur burial chamber.

a substantial woollen industry. By the beginning of the 15th century there was an estimated population of a thousand. However, the borough soon began to decline, possibly due to the silting up of the estuary, although plague has also been blamed. As Newport dwindled in size and population, so the story grew of a 'lost town' on the coast — inspired by the old Welsh name, Trefdraeth, 'town on the sands' — but this is nothing more than a folk-memory of the original extent of the Medieval borough.

The Castle still dominates the town from its hill-top site. The norman ringwork was crowned with a thin masonry wall in the early 13th century, later supplemented with three large towers of different size. In the 16th century the decaying fortress

passed to the Owens of Henllys, and was described by the historian George as '*a stronge and lardge castle, moted, garretted, and with towres, and having a lardge courte within*'. In 1859 the ruined gatehouse was converted into a house, which remains in private occupation to this day.

The parish church of St Martin stands across the road opposite the castle. This Medieval cruci-form building, twice restored (drastically) by the Victorians, may have replaced an earlier church dedicated to St Curig. A 7th–9th-century cross stone was found in a nearby hedge and moved into the church for safe keeping. Follow the lane uphill past the church, to where you will see a moss-covered ring of boulders enclosing a riverside spring. This is St Curig's well, further evidence to suggest a pre-Norman origin for the church.

Back in town, there is one more monument worthy of notice: **Carreg Coetan** burial chamber. This Neolithic tomb now lies surrounded by modern housing, just off the road to Pen y Bont. The cairn has been robbed of stone, leaving the megalithic chamber standing in splendid isolation. Only two out of the four remaining uprights support the 10 foot long capstone.

CERRIG Y GOF (66)

This is probably the oddest of the Neolithic tombs found in the Nevern valley. The site lies on the right-hand side of the Fishguard road, 1½ miles west of Newport. Cerrig y Gof ('the blacksmith's stones') is a group of five small burial chambers arranged haphazardly around the edge of an oval mound. The site was excavated by Fenton who found potsherds, charcoal, bone fragments, and many black sea pebbles — perhaps placed there as votive offerings.

CARN INGLI (67)

This great rocky crag frowning down on the clustered rooftops of Newport is the site of one of the largest stone-built hillforts in wales. The name derives from the Latin *mons angelorum*, 'the mountain of angels', after a legend which tells of St Brynach ascending to the highest peak to discourse with the angels. Numerous paths lead across the common to the Iron Age fort, which occupies the summit of this jagged rock outcrop. Although the defensive walls survive mostly as heaps of tumbled stones, the plan can still be traced. Solid drystone walls divide up the summit into four enclosures, with an outer line of defence on the lower west and north slopes. There are no less than twelve entrances to the fort, all simple (but easily defendable) gaps through the thick walls. The foundations of between 20-30 round huts remain, along with a number of curious platforms and enclosures, which may have been filled with earth for use as gardens or cultivation plots.

Cerrig y Gof burial chambers.

Llanfihangel Abercywyn Church.

Laugharne Castle.

Early dwelling sites on Carn Ingli common are not confined solely to the shelter of the great hill-fort. Dozens of huts, pens and drystone enclosures lie scattered over the common, but it is impossible to be certain of their age. Most probably date from the Roman period, when the tribes of west Wales were encouraged — or forced — out of their strongholds by the Romans. But there are many other undateable mounds and stone settings, some, like Carn Briw, undoubtedly the burial mounds of the Bronze Age élite. The Bronze Age is also the period to which **Bedd Morris** standing stone (68) belongs. This fine monolith is conveniently sited next to the mountain road from Pontfaen to Newport. Folk-tales claim that this Prehistoric ritual monument is the gravestone of either a high-wayman, or the loser in a duel. A more unusual tradition is associated with the **Lady Stone (69)** on the main Newport to Fishguard road, quarter of a mile east of the Llanllawer turning. This stone, too, lies next to the road, and has been incorporated into a hedge. The 9 foot-high slab is said to resemble a veiled woman, and it was the custom of travellers in earlier days to salute the stone by raising their hats. Could this be a folk-memory enshrined and distorted in legend of the veneration and rituals performed before this stone idol of the Bronze Age tribes?

LLANLLAWER (70)

The existing church of Llanllawer was entirely rebuilt in 1860, but two cross stones of 7th-9th century date have been set into the gateposts, perhaps to prevent evil spirits from entering the churchyard. In a field beside the church stands a large and impressive holy well. The spring water once had a 'reputation of the most miraculous efficacy in various disorders', but it is now dry, although the covering vault has recently been restored. Yet the waters had a more sinister attri-bute, for Ffynnon Gapan, Llanllawer, was a 'cursing well'; while good wishes were granted by casting in straight pins, a bent pin dropped into the water was said to fulfil evil thoughts.

Beside a lane ¾ mile east of Llanllawer is the remains of the most impressive stone row in west Wales. This is the ominously named Parc y Meirw, 'field of the dead', and four large megaliths survive upstanding out of an original alignment of eight. A neolithic burial chamber known as Coitan Arthur

Llanllawer; the cursing well.

once stood nearby, but in 1844 the landowner broke up the stones for building materials. As might be expected, ill-luck befell the vandal for his rash act.

LLANYCHAER, LLANYCHLWYDOG AND PONTFAEN CHURCHES (71-73)

These three parish churches nestle on the wooded slopes of the Gwaun valley, which winds its way inland amongst outliers of the Preseli Mountains. Although the buildings are modern in fabric, they retain stone memorials of their Dark Age predecessors.

Near the entrance to the valley is **Llanychaer (71)**, entirely rebuilt in 1876, but containing a cross inscribed stone of 600-800 AD. Another stone (now lost, but fortunately recorded by the antiquarian Edward Lhwyd in 1698) carried a Latin inscription commemorating *Macedeccetus, son of Eorocass.* A few miles further up the valley stands the Victorian church of **Llanychlwydog (72)**, one of the least pronounceable place-names in Wales. The building has recently been converted into a private dwelling and, prior to that, the Dyfed Archaeolo-gical Trust carried out a small-scale excavation to discover the foundations of the Medieval church. The church had been built on an earlier cemetery, fragments of bone from a grave were radio-carbon dated to the 9th century. Four 7th-9th century cros-ses also survive. Two similar crosses can be seen beside the entrance to nearby **Pontfaen (73)** church, on the opposite side of the valley.

Apart from ecclesiastical monuments, there are several Iron Age hillforts in the Gwaun valley, as well as early domestic buildings such as Kilkiffeth, home of 'the kings of the mountains', and **Garn**, a Medieval hall-house with a conical chimney (a rare upland survivor of this distinctive southern feature).

THE PRESELI MOUNTAINS (74-77)

We now move to the bleak heights of the Preseli Mountains, an upland area nowhere over 1300 feet, but nevertheless potentially treacherous. Anyone intent on exploring the rich archaeological heritage of this bleakly beautiful area of west Wales should go armed with a decent map, compass and hiking boots. In fact and legend the peaks of the Preselis figure predominantly in our history, but the great number of upland archaeological sites here should not be seen on their own; for many other Prehistoric monuments in the surrounding countryside (such as 63, 64, 78) are extensions of the main Preseli group.

The Bronze Age hierarchy were privileged indeed to be buried in cairns on the summits of the highest peaks for miles around. Burial mounds can be visited on Foeleryr, Foel-cwmcerwyn and Foel-feddau, with outliers at Mynydd Cilciffeth in the west, and Y Frenni Fawr (58) in the east.

CERRIG MEIBION ARTHUR (74)

On the north side of the mountain road from Mynachlog-ddu to Rosebush, about 3 miles north-east of Maenclochog, is this fine megalith group, Cerrig Meibion Arthur, 'the stones of Arthur's sons'. The name alludes to an episode in King Arthur's hunt of a wild boar, recounted in the Welsh folk-tales, *The Mabinogion*. The king's son, Gwydre, was among those killed by the boar in a skirmish on a nearby mountaintop. This area of Wales has a surprising number of Prehistoric monuments and natural features named after that semi-legendary king, all of which existed long before Arthur's time. This is true of Cerrig Meibion Arthur, for these two tall standing stones were set up as part of a ritual centre in the Bronze Age, at least 3000 years ago.

GORS FAWR (75)

The Bronze Age is also the period to which the Gors Fawr stone circle belongs. This lies in a field off the road from Mynachlog-ddu to Llangolman,

about 1½ miles south-east of the above site. Although the remains are fairly unimpressive, and will probably disappoint visitors expecting to see towering megaliths, this is nevertheless one of the most complete circles in Wales. There are 16 stones arranged in an oval ring, 70-74 feet across, with two taller outlying stones some 440 feet away to the north-east.

Earlier this century a local minister-cum-archaeologist, Done Bushell, claimed that there were at least eight stone circles in the Preseli district. Some have now been destroyed, while others such as Bedd Arthur (76) and the Dyffryn cairn (82) do not belong in the same class of monument as Gors Fawr. This area was of undeniable importance to Prehistoric Man, yet Bushell (like many antiquarians before him) used a little too much imagination when viewing the scattered rocks and boulders of this rugged landscape.

Cerrig Meibion Arthur standing stones.

66

Gors Fawr stone circle.

BEDD ARTHUR (76)

Like Gors Fawr, the stone 'circle' at Bedd Arthur is something of an initial disappointment, for none of the stones is more than three feet high; but the location is superb, and the views on a clear day make the long climb to the site well worth the effort. The easiest and quickest way to get to Bedd Arthur is along Talymynydd from the mountain road at Glynsaithmaen. As with other similarly named monuments, this has nothing to do with king Arthur, and was probably a Bronze Age ritual site. Twelve stones remain out of a probable eighteen originally, arranged in an oval formation.

In full sight from Bedd Arthur is the saw-toothed backdrop of **Carn Meini** which, although possessing no genuine monument, is included here for its association with the most famous of all stone circles. Over 4000 years ago countless Neolithic labourers hauled away great slabs of spotted dolerite, or 'bluestone', from this outcrop, to be taken on a 240-mile journey to Salisbury Plain where they formed part of the megalithic complex now known as Stonehenge. Skill, brute force and sheer determination were the main factors in obtaining this speckled rock, although the 12th-century writer, Geoffrey of Monmouth, gave a more magical explanation for the building of

Stonehenge. In his book 'The History of the Kings of Britain', Geoffrey claims that the wizard Merlin used his powers to transport the stones from Ireland, to be reassembled as a monument to over 400 britons killed by the Saxons. 'These stones are connected with certain secret religious rites and they have various properties which are medicinally important', claimed the wizard.

FOELDRYGARN (77)

About a mile beyond Carn Meini, the mountain once more breaks out in a rugged outcrop, the 'bare hill of the three cairns': Foeldrygarn. This is an aptly named site, for within this trivallate hillfort rise the domed profiles of three large Bronze Age burial mounds. The hillfort came later, and it may have been occupied into the Roman period. The pock-marked hut foundations of over 200 dwellings can be traced on the rocky hilltop, most situated within the area of the drystone ramparts. In contrast to this massive, 11-acre site, the nearby fort at **Carn Ffoi** is a diminutive, but equally strongly defended settlement. The area enclosed by the drystone rampart is small, but the defences were nevertheless very elaborate, with a well-defined *chevaux-de-frise* leading to a bottleneck entrance — all designed to deter a cavalry charge.

BUARTH ARTHUR (78)

Yet another Arthurian misnomer, and one of the earliest recorded ancient monuments in west Wales. It was known to the antiquarian Edward Lhwyd (d. 1709), and Daniel Defoe, writing in about 1725, described it as a 'a circle of mighty stones, very much like Stone-henge in Wiltshire . . . and tho' the people call it Buarth Arthur, or King Arthur's throne, we see no reason to believe that King Arthur knew anything of it'. Defoe was right of course, for this is an Early Bronze Age ritual monument, but alas, since the 18th century many of the encircling stones have been robbed, and now only two remain. Buarth Arthur lies in a field behind a modern bungalow at Groesffordd on the A478, roughly halfway between Llandissilio and Crymmyrch. We are, in fact, back in the old county of Carmarthenshire, but the complex of monuments at Groesffordd must be seen as outliers of the Preseli group. Buarth Arthur, or Meini Gwyr, is an embanked stone circle, which originally consisted of 17 standing stones set into the inner face of a circular enclosure, 120 feet across. The monument appears to have gone out of use by the Middle Bronze Age, since excavation revealed that one of the stones had been disturbed by the construction of a hearth of that date.

Buarth Arthur is only one of many Prehistoric monuments in this area; there are at least 12 cairns here, although only a few are immediately apparent.

Two standing stones, known as Yr Allor, 'the altar', are found 250 yards west of the circle. A third stone has been removed, and although this is claimed to be the remains of a cromlech, the stones are more likely to have been part of a larger mega-lithic complex associated with the circle. The same uncertainty rests with **Castell Garw** enclosure, about 400 yards beyond the junction on the right-hand side of the road. This has every appearance of being a hillslope enclosure of Iron Age date, but there is a strong tradition that several large stones were removed from here, making it likely that Castell Garw is another 'ritual circle'. A short distance further along the road to Crymmyrch, a jumble of stones on the left marks the remains of another Prehistoric relic, in this case a Neolithic chambered tomb, **Carn Besi**.

GWAL Y FILIAST (79)

In a sheltered grove of beech trees on the banks of the river Taf stands the fine Neolithic tomb known as Gwal y Filiast, or Bwrdd Arthur. The site can be reached by following the disused railway line south from Llanglydwen village, for about ¾ mile. The massive capstone is almost 12 feet long and is supported by four remaining slabs; a fifth supporter lies nearby. The tomb was said to have been surrounded by a ring of 32 stones, now marked by a line of trees. Nothing remains of this circle today, which may have been the kerb of a vanished round cairn.

LLANDEILO LLWYDARTH (80)

About 1¼ miles east of Maenclochog, beside the road to Llangolman, stands the crumbling remains of the parish church of St Teilo. The building has been ruined for well over 100 years, and lies in a field at the back of Llandeilo farm. Two inscribed stones of 5th or early 6th century date formerly stood by the entrance, and indicate that the existing Medieval church occupies the site of an Early Christian burial ground. The inscriptions on the stones commemorate Andagellus and Coimagnus, sons of Cavetus; Andagellus' son, Curgagnus, is named on the 6th-century stone at Cenarth (24), which originally stood at nearby Temple Druid. Both stones have been removed for safe keeping to Maenclochog church, and indicate that Llandeilo was the family 'mausoleum' of local dignitaries who lived and died in this area over 14 centuries ago.

North-east of the old church is a modern brick pump-house on the site of St Teilo's holy well, which once had a widespread reputation for curing pulmonary complaints, tuberculosis and whooping cough. For the healing power to be effective the water had to be drunk early in the morning out of 'Penglog Teilo' — part of a human skull, said to be a relic of the saint. The cup-shaped skull, burnished through constant use, was filled and handed to the pilgrim only by the senior living member of the Melchior family (previous owners of the farm, and hereditary keepers of the skull). Even in this century people drank the water this way, and made votive offerings of pins to end hostilities in the First World War.

NEW MOAT (81)

A sign on the green proudly announces New Moat as 'the best kept village in Dyfed, 1977', and, arguably, it still deserves that title. The current building craze has yet to hit New Moat and so this sleepy hamlet has hardly grown beyond its Medieval extent. The OS map optimistically marks the castle earthworks as a 'Roman camp', but the town grew up in the shelter of a 12th-century motte and bailey castle, one of a string of Norman fortifications north of the Landsker. A document of c. 1200 refers to 'a burgage by the east gate', and so the early settlement may have been walled, or else located within the large bailey. Later in the 13th century the manor of New Moat was expanded and developed by the Bishops of St David's into a sizeable borough.

All that now survives is the rugged tower of the Medieval parish church (the rest was rebuilt in the last century), and the impressive motte and bailey. The tree-covered mound is over 30 feet high and is

New Moat; the parish church.

still surrounded by a water-filled moat. On one side of the ditch is a stone sluice for regulating the height of the water, but this may be a later feature. A monument within the church commemorates the Scourfield family, whose nearby ruined mansion Fenton saw in the early 19th century. According to tradition the Scourfield's riches were gained at a dog race, hence the nimble greyhounds adorning their coat of arms.

HENRY'S MOAT (82)

This place-name has been interpreted as Castell Hen Dre, 'castle of the old town', i.e. the forerunner of nearby 'New' Moat. Henry's Moat is a cluster of farms, a church and some inconspicuous earthworks on a hillside three miles west of Maenclochog. In plan, the austere church is off-balanced by a large south transept, and the extensive Victorian restoration work was not helped much. Behind the graveyard is a damaged 15 foot-high motte, while a short distance south is a roadside Iron Age hillfort, now poorly preserved although the single low rampart can just be traced.

Further east along the Maenclochog road are two monuments of contrasting age but similar in function; both were constructed to serve religious needs. At the rear of Bernard's Well farm is a marshy hollow marking the site of **St Brynach's holy well**. At the beginning of the 19th century, Fenton saw a ruined chapel here, and a 7th-9th-century cross stone, but only the spring remains today. A short distance to the north-east is the **Dyffryn cairn circle**, which can be reached along a muddy track from Budloy farm (ask for permission to visit the site at the farm). This is a truely impressive cairn, for the central mound was encircled by a kerb of megalithic proportions. There appears to have been about 26 stones in the circle, but only 10 remain standing today, the tallest about 7 feet high.

CASTLEBYTHE (83)

This is another Preseli village which grew up around a Norman castle. Castlebythe lies just over a mile north-west of Henry's Moat, and the tree-covered motte and bailey can be seen beside the road on the east side of the village. The summit of the adjacent mountain is crowned by two large Bronze Age cairns, while on the slopes overlooking the village is Cas-fuwch, a defended Iron Age settlement. Although the outer ditch has silted up, the line of the defensive rampart is complete except for a gap on the south-west side.

CASTLE FLEMISH (84)

Less than two miles south-west of Castlebythe stands the earthwork remains of Castle Flemish, a notorious misnomer, for this is neither a castle nor of Flemish work. The site has been damaged by a minor road from Wolf's Castle to Henry's Moat, which at least allows a closer inspection of the surviving earthworks. Castle Flemish has long been identified as the Roman fort of *Ad Vigesimum* listed in a transcribed 14th-century manuscript of one 'Richard of Cirencester'. Unfortunately, this manuscript is a spurious 18th-century concoction, and there is no solid evidence to prove that the Romans ever established anything further west of Carmarthen. Castle Flemish undoubtedly represents a native farmstead modelled along Roman lines, like Cwmbrwyn (38) and Trelissey (41). When Sir Mortimer Wheeler excavated the site in 1922, he found Roman-type bricks, flue tiles, hexagonal roofing tiles, and imported pottery. This evidence suggested an occupation date in the first and early second century AD. A section was also cut through the defences, which consist of a rectangular enclosure surrunded by a revetted bank and 7 foot-deep ditch. The existence of a second Romano-British 'villa' in this area is attested by Fenton, who saw 'great quantities of bricks of various size and shape' in a field west of Wolf's Castle. Workmen digging out a hedge in 1806 uncovered the bricks along with the foundations of a hypocaust (underfloor heating), which may have formed part of a bath-house.

CARN TURNE BURIAL CHAMBER (85)

Although the great chamber has collapsed, and the surrounding cairn mound robbed, the Neolithic tomb at Carn Turne is nevertheless one of the most impressive sites in west Wales. Like Pentre Ifan (62), Carn Turne is a portal tomb with a facade of upright slabs defining the entrance approach. The

Carn Turne burial chamber and standing stone.

18 foot-long capstone has fallen, but six stones of the funnel-shaped facade remain upright. There is a slender monolith a little to the south. The site lies next to the Ambleston to St Dogwells road, about ½ miles north-east of Wolf's castle. A gate in the roadside hedge leads on to the moor where the tomb is situated. Not far away to the south-east is the Parc y Llyn burial chamber, partly incorporated into a field wall, but just visible from the roadside. A third ruined tomb at nearby Colston farm further testifies to the presence of the Neolithic tribes in this area.

SPITTAL (86)

The village of Spittal takes its name from a 'hospital', or hospice, for poor pilgrims and wayfarers built in 1293 by Bishop Bek of St David's. The Dissolutiuon put paid to that noble establishment, and until 1870 some fragments of walls survived of the building. In 1572 three local men, acting on information received from a Carmarthenshire priest, discovered a brass pot containing gold and silver at the hospice ruins. Unfortunately, the Sheriff of Pembroke got wind of the affair, but wrote that the full story would never be learned without the parties being 'menaced with some torture'. The outcome is not recorded, but it is puzzling how the priest found out about the treasure. Had he hidden it at the Dissolution, and was only then attempting to reclaim it with the connivance of three blundering accomplices? We may never know.

The Medieval parish church contains a 5th-early 6th-century inscribed stone commemorating *Evalus, son of Dencus*; an additional line informs us that the monument was set up by his mother. A short distance east along the Scolton road is the overgrown earthworks of an Iron Age hillfort, the the original settlement here.

CASTELL BUCKETTE (87)

Although on private land and not normally accessible to the public, this intriguing site is just visible from the roadside off the A40, 1 mile north-east of Letterston. Castell Buckette is an Iron Age defended settlement which consists of an inner bank and ditch enclosure, with an entrance and annexe on the west side. An outer enclosure survives on the south and west sides incorporated into a field boundary. The site was once thought to be a Neolithic or Bronze Age ritual enclosure, but is now rightly identified as a typical Iron Age settlement site. This is further confirmed by the recent discovery of an Iron Age cremation burial just outside the ramparts. However, since the bones were those of animals and humans, the deposit may not represent a conventional burial. A macabre theory offered by the excavator suggests that the 'burial' was the remains of a cannibalistic ritual feast.

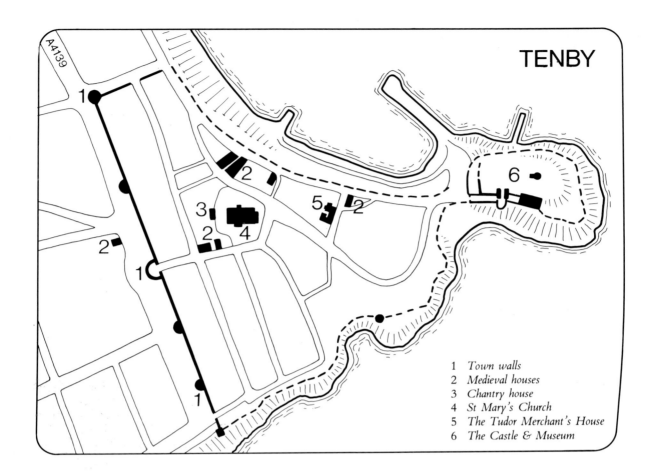

1 Town walls
2 Medieval houses
3 Chantry house
4 St Mary's Church
5 The Tudor Merchant's House
6 The Castle & Museum

Tenby, Pembroke and the Castlemartin Peninsula

(Sites 88–114)

TENBY (88)

Tenby requires a guidebook by itself to do justice to the wealth of historic and interesting places, only a few of which can be described here. This is arguably the most popular of the historic towns of west Wales, even though some of its character is periodically lost under a welter of garish souvenir shops.

Firmly clasped by the powerful Medieval walls, the fortified old town is a veritable warren of winding streets and narrow lanes, where a scatter of architectural features attempt to hide under rendered walls and modern shop facades. Blocked doorways and Medieval windows can be seen in the walls of the Regent Restaurant (St George's Street) and the Merchant's Cottage (Quay Street), while the Plantagenet Restaurant (also Quay Street) contains two recently discovered wall paintings. The alley behind the Sun Inn (High Street) is overshadowed by rows of massive stone corbels, and two tall 'Flemish' round chimneys huddle at the rear of a house just opposite the Five Arches gate. All these features proclaim to the observant visitor the rich architectural heritage of the town.

Beyond the Medieval walls, in the direction of Norton, stood the hospital of St John and the leper house of 'Saint Mayre Mawdlyn'. Both were dissolved in 1547, although St John's was later rebuilt as a mansion. Nothing remains of this house today, nor of 'White's House', a late Medieval building with a splendid Renaissance doorway. This stood between the church and High Street, and was the home of mayor Thomas White who, in 1471, aided the young Henry Tudor to flee to Brittany, following the Lancastrian defeat at Tewkesbury. Tomb-effigies of White and his son are to be found inside the majestic parish church, a useful starting point for any historical exploration of the town.

St Mary's Church

Dominating the town, and a landmark for miles out to sea, is the 152 feet-high tower and spire of the parish church. This large and resplendent building has a complex architectural history, and the existing structure is the culmination of almost three centuries of rebuilding and extension. The earliest masonry (13th-century) is incorporated into the nave, which was later 'sandwiched' between north and south aisles. The chancel and tower also date from the 13th century, although the former was extended and re-roofed in the 15th century. The much repaired spire is another late Medieval addition, so too is the panelled waggon roof of the nave an chancel, richly decorated with painted figures and bosses carved into a variety of patterns — foliage, leering faces, dragons, mer-maids and fishes. Among the numerous monuments within the church worth highlighting are the garish, near life-sized figures of Thomas and Margaret ap Rhys of Scotsborough (89), and tomb-effigies of a finely dressed 14th-century lady, and an emaciated cadaver — a grim reminder of the transient pleasures of life.

A few yards west of the church is a meagre, but highly-decorated fragment of a late 15th-century building, traditionally known as a Carmelite friary, but more probably a dwelling for chantry priests.

On the headland below the town stands the remains of **Tenby castle**, the *raison d'être* for the development of the Medieval town. This was once a native Dark Age stronghold, 'a fine fortress, sea encircled' as a 9th-century poet described it, and the Normans established one of their frontier castles here in the late 11th or early 12th century. The existing stonework is much later, probably the work of William de Valance, Earl of Pembroke,

Tenby; the parish church of St. Mary.

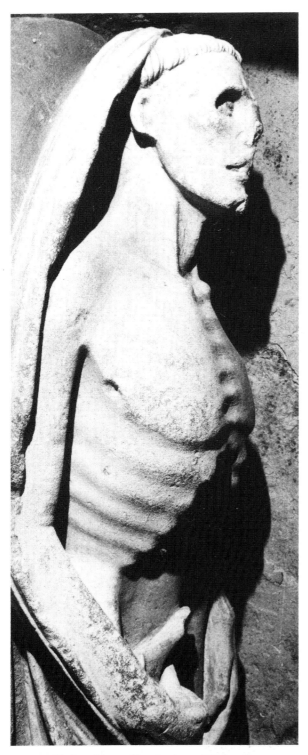

Tenby; skinny effigy in the parish church.

who also began work on a fortified wall to enclose and protect the clifftop town. This wall was repaired by a later Earl of Pembroke, Jasper Tudor, in the 1450s, and was again patched up in 1588 during the Armada scare. Only one of the three original gateways survives, the well-known 'Five Arches' — a D-shaped barbican covering the south gate. During the Civil War the castle was held for the king, and suffered heavy bombardment from sea before capitulating. Only a few shattered walls and a gatehouse (a smaller version of the Five Arches) survive. Part of the castle was rebuilt as a museum, which now houses an important collection of finds from Caldey (14) and Hoyle's Mouth cave (92).

During the later Middle Ages and early post-Reformation period Tenby was a flourishing port, but plague contributed to its decline in the 17th century, and as late as the last century, large areas were derelict and uninhabited. The town has now recovered much of its former prosperity, and has grown far beyond the limits of the Medieval walls. The most notable suriving domestic building is the late 15th-century **'Tudor Merchant's House'** in Quay Street. The plain and rugged stonework of the house is in stark contrast to the rendered and modern-looking buildings nearby, but the adjoining Plantagenet Restaurant (which has a huge projecting fireplace at the rear) and the kitchen wing of the Pam-Pam Restaurant incorporate work of a similar age.

The 'Merchant's House' has been in the care of the National Trust since 1939, and is open to the public from Easter to September. On the left upon entering is a partitioned-off chamber which may have been a shop or workroom. There are remains of painted decorations on the plastered walls, but their age is uncertain. The two upper floors of the house are now reached by modern stairs, but a blocked door in the north wall indicates that the first floor was originally reached by an outside flight of steps (see cutaway drawing). Renovation work in 1984 enabled limited excavations of the interior to be carried out, including a scientific examination of the contents of the cess-pit. This ostensibly unsavoury work nevertheless provided a valuable insight into the eating habits and economic condition of the Tudor occupants of the house. The garderobe has ceased to be used at some time in the 17th or 18th century, as it had been

Tenby; the 'Five Arches' gate.

back-filled with rubble containing potsherds of that period. These potsherds highlight Tenby's former maritime trade. Most of the sherds came from vessels of north Devon manufacture, although a few originated in Spain or Portugal. Fruit pips and stones, cereals and fish bones indicated a varied diet, but behind the good food and affluent lifestyle there was the reality of Medieval hygiene: the cess-pit is located right next to the kitchen, and even if it was sealed with a stout door, the atmosphere could hardly have been very pleasant. Cinders and charcoal found in the pit were probably thrown in to dampen the odour. The occupants were riddled with intestinal worms, and had to make do with hay or wool for toilet paper, and the presence of rat bones indicate that this disease-carrying mammal was a frequent house guest in 16th-century Tenby.

SCOTSBOROUGH HOUSE (89)

Visitors leaving Tenby along the B4318 to Carew pass by the remains of one of the most complex and intriguing late-Medieval gentry houses in the county. There is no signpost to point the way to Scotsborough, nor are the ruins visible from the road, yet despite the passage of time and the inevitable encroachment of undergrowth, a substantial portion of the building survives. The house can be reached along a public footpath which leaves a lay-by on the B4318, ¾ mile west of Tenby.

This was the dwelling of the Scotsborough Perrots, the most important branch of that large Pembrokeshire family, who acquired the property in the early 15th century. In 1614 the house passed to the Ap Rhys family of Rickeston, the first of many successive owners, and by the 19th century only the west wing (converted into cottages) was inhabited. A smallpox epidemic there in 1824 drove out the

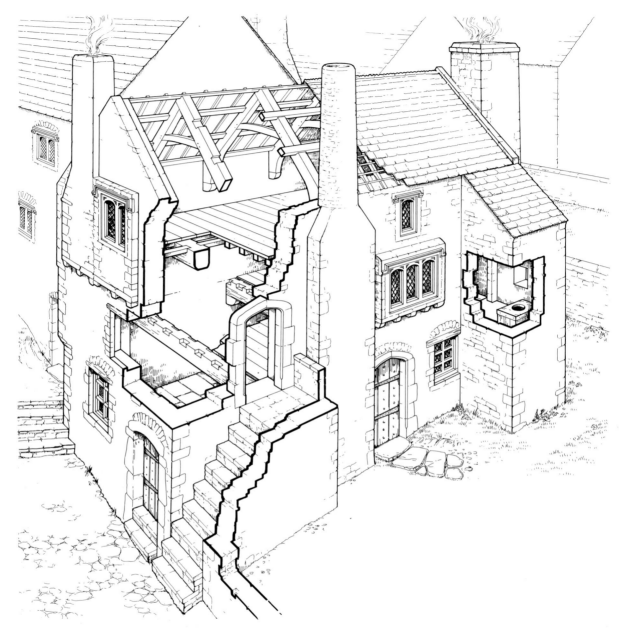

Tenby; cutaway reconstruction of the 16th century Merchant's House.

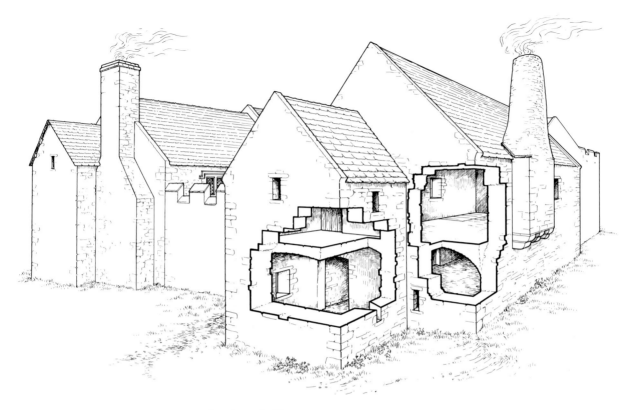

Scotsborough House; a cutaway reconstruction.

remaining inhabitants, an event which fostered the belief that Scotsborough was 'an accursed place'.

The remains comprise a U-shaped building of three distinct phases, mainly of 15th-16th-century date, with later stables and outbuildings on one side. The most remarkable part of the house is undoubtedly the east wing, which has a vaulted basement and a first-floor hall. Compared with other similar Pembrokeshire buildings this should be the earliest part of the house, but in fact it appears to have been the last major addition (since the walls abut against the rest of the house). The hall was a gloomy and oppressive room, warmed by a large fireplace, but lit only by narrow, unglazed loopholes; the building was, in effect, a small fortified residence which had been added to an earlier, undefended mansion. At a later stage (probably during the Civil War) the house was enclosed on the north and east sides by a fortified wall pierced with triangular gun loops, of a type still to be seen at Manorbier Castle (96). In 1906 the remains were cleared and a survey made of the building. Today

the undergrowth has reclaimed Scotsbourough, so that the whole site has the appearance of a Peruvian ruin deep in some impenetrable jungle. Spring or early summer is the best time to visit gloomy Scotsborough.

GUMFRESTON CHURCH (90)

About half a mile beyond Scotsborough a small sign points the way to St Lawrence's Church, Gumfreston, a peaceful and secluded building hidden away in a wooded dell below the road. Beside the churchyard gate is a ruined and overgrown 'Priest's' house which was used as a schoolroom in the last century. The parish church is now entered through a large porch on the west, but the original doorway was in the middle of the nave wall on the south; its filled-in outline can be seen from the outside. The interior of this 13th-14th-century building is severely plain, and the only ornamentation is the tiny rib-vault in the south chapel, and the remains of mural decorations in the

Gumfreston; the parish church of St. Lawrence.

nave. The crude paintings are believed to represent implements of torture associated with the martyrdom of Gumfreston's patron saint. The vaulted ground floor of the tall 15th-century tower acts as a north transept, and beside the chancel arch is a blocked doorway which formerly led up to the rood loft.

An early 19th-century traveller justly praised Gumfreston as 'an oasis in this dusty world, and the waters of life flow forth here for the benefit of him . . . who visits this retired yet cheerful spot'. This is a reference to the three bubbling wells below the church. The chalybeate waters were formerly held in great repute for their medicinal qualities, and on Easter Day local people would visit the wells to drop bent pins in as votive offerings, a pactice called 'throwing Lent away'.

ST FLORENCE (91)

West of Tenby, the marshy course of the silted-up Ritec river winds inland to the little village of St Florence, clustered about the graveyard of the tall towered Medieval church. The village is a pleasing mixture of old and new. When Fenton visited St Florence in the early 19th century he commented on 'the many ruinous houses and fragments of walls', and believed the village 'to have been much more populous than it now is'; but this picture of decay no longer holds true.

The village is dominated by the 14th-century parish church, a splendid and little-restored cruciform building with a chancel, nave, twin transepts and a side chapel. The vaulted south transept is, in fact, the ground floor of the 15th-century tower, from which a low passage-squint opens into the aisled chancel. Above the chancel arch can be seen the corbels which once supported the rood-loft. Further evidence of the village's Medieval origin is indicated by two surviving 'Flemish' chimneys — one below the church having outlived the house for which it was built, while the other is still attached to a much-restored Medieval house. Fenton also mentioned that the vicarage stable (once a dwelling) had a vaulted roof, another common architectural feature in this part of west Wales.

Still on the theme of domestic architecture, at

78

West Tarr and Carswell, east of the village, are the remains of late Medieval buildings. Both are intermediary types between the first-floor hall and the tower house, having the main domestic room above a vaulted ground floor, and reached only by a removable ladder. These buildings have the vastly scaled-down proportions of a church or castle tower. At **West Tarr** the house is built out onto a sloping hillside, and has vaults on both floors. A blocked doorway on the south side indicates the position of the original first-floor entrance. Two other tower-like buildings (including a privy) are similarly built against the adjacent slopes. At **Carswell** (on private land) domesticity played a larger role than defence, and the vaulted

ground floor is provided with a huge kitchen fireplace. The hall itself was heated by a smaller fireplace contained within a massive projecting chimney. The only communication between the hall and kitchen was by an external stairway, so we can imagine that few meals were served piping hot to the occupants of Carswell.

HOYLE'S MOUTH (92)

Hoyle's Mouth cave, or the Hoyle (a derivation of *hole*), lies 1½ miles south-west of Tenby in a wooded hillside overlooking the Ritec valley. It can be reached by following the A4139 to Pembroke, turning right opposite a service station, and then right again along a minor road. After a short

Carswell, St. Florence; cutaway view of the tower house.

distance a signposted track on the left leads up to the cave. A torch is needed for a full exploration of the cave, which consists of a narrow, twisting passage with a few small chambers. This was a popular place for Victorians to visit, and one 19th-century guidebook described the Hoyle as 'beautifully adorned by stalactites, in some places clustering like grapes and acorns of frosted silver, or pendant from the roof like huge icicles', a description which unfortunately bears little resemblance to the cave today.

Hoyle's Mouth is an important archaeological site, and for this reason finds a place in this book. The cave has been excavated several times, the first recorded dig in 1840 by the Rev. G. N. Smith, rector of Gumfreston, and the last in 1964. Finds from the various excavations include Prehistoric flint implements, animal bones, and Iron Age and Romano-British potsherds. There were numerous remains of Ice Age animals, including mammoth, reindeer and woolly rhinocerous, brought into the cave by carnivorous tenants such as wolf and hyaena. Some of the flint tools discovered in the 19th century are now considered to belong to the Late Upper Palaeolithic period, and were painstakingly shaped by hunters who sheltered in the cave, soon after the last Ice Age.

Hoyle's Mouth has some literary fame as well, for it has been identified as the model for Belarius' cave in Shakespeare's 'Cymbeline'. The brief descriptions in the play correspond strikingly to Hoyle's Mouth and the locale, although just how the Great Bard ever got to hear about this cave is never made clear. There is also a less believable story of a dog which entered a passage in the Wogan Cave, Pembroke Castle (101) and eventually emerged from a crevice at the end of the Hoyle. Unfortunately for the story, there is no way on from that crevice, as any slim visitor may care to find out.

A short distance away to the south is the less accessible Little Hoyle, or Longbury Bank cave. This shorter cave has recently been excavated, and the discovery of Roman, Dark Age and Medieval potsherds suggests that there was a settlement in the vicinity, perhaps on the hilltop above the cave. A small cross carved into the calcite-covered wall of the cave may have been the work of an Early Christian hermit.

PENALLY CHURCH (93)

The presence of Early Christians in this part of west Wales is further attested by the rich legacy of sculptured stones at Penally, one mile south-west of Tenby. In the Dark Ages a native monastery was established here by the great St Teilo (who is reputed to be buried here), but the existing church is an imposing, cruciform edifice of 14th-century date. The tall, thin battlemented tower is an addition of the 15th or 16th century. The dimly-lit interior is roofed with plain pointed vaults, and the south transept holds a treasure trove of decorated stone monuments. The finest is undoubtedly an

Penally Cross.

Porth y Rhaw promontory fort.

Flimston Medieval House.

Manorbier Castle.

Coetan Arthur, St. David's.

early 10th-century wheel-cross encrusted with plait, key and twisting vine motifs, which rivalls the great crosses at Carew (99) and Nevern (61) in complexity of design. Another richly-carved slab is all that remains of a similar cross, while a third monument, inscribed with the Latin words *'this is the cross which Mail Domnac erected'*, is unfortunately lost. A tomb recess on the east side of the transept contains two 13th-century partial effigies of members of the De Naunton family.

There is another site of historical interest in Penally village, the misnamed 'St Deniol's Chapel', in the grounds of Abbey House, 200 yards north of the church. Despite a tradition of an ecclesiastical origin, the 'chapel' is clearly a late Medieval domestic building, which was adapted as a gazebo in the 18th or early 19th century. In plan, the building comprises an L-shaped range with a first-floor hall above a vaulted basement. The main room was heated by a large fireplace which still retains its distinctive 'Flemish' round chimney. The building can adequately be seen from the roadside, although customers of the Abbey House tea rooms are usually permitted to explore the ruins.

CALDEY ISLAND (94)

Caldey Island, in Welsh Ynys Pŷr, lies two miles south of Tenby, and is a popular venue for summer visitors to this part of Wales. Between June and September a fleet of little boats regularly deposit daytrippers on this island, which has formed a retreat for Man since ancient times.

From the discovery of numerous Mesolithic flint implements we know that Caldey was inhabited at least 8000 years ago by an industrious group of tool makers, who established a 'factory' on the eastern tip of the island. Of course, Caldey was not an island then, but a rocky plateau overlooking a broad coastal plain, for the post-glacial sea level had not then reached its present height. From the 19th century onwards periodic excavations of the limestones caves on the north-east side of the island have revealed the bones of extinct animals such as mammoth, rhinoceros, reindeer, giant deer and cave lion, and also Mesolithic flints and Neolithic potsherds. The flint tool 'production line' at Daylight Rock left over 7400 implements and worked debris for archaeologists to find thousands of years later and, from Nanna's Cave alone came evidence of periodic occupation by Man in the Upper Paleolithic, Neolithic, late Bronze/early Iron Age and the Roman period.

Despite their importance, the bone caves are not normally accessible to visitors, and the most noteworthy above-ground monuments are those buildings associated with the island's rich Christian heritage. Long after the cave dwellers left Caldey, the island was used as a retreat by Early Christian saints and holy men. Saints David, Gildas and Illtyd were reputed visitors to this remote chunk of land, but the early monastery is more closely associated with St Samson, who replaced the drunkard Piro as Abbot in the 6th century. Such a native monastery did not long survive the arrival of the Normans, and in the early 12th century it was re-established along lines more familiar to the invaders, as a priory cell of St Dogmael's (28). At the Dissolution the priory was closed, the monks evicted and the estate sold off; but the wheel has turned full circle, and Caldey is once more owned by a community of monks.

Visitors to Caldey have first to run the gauntlet of tasteless and garish souvenir shops before experiencing something of the tranquility of this island retreat. The 'village' post office should not be missed, however, for it contains a small exhibition of Prehistoric finds. From the magnificent modern Abbey a wooded track leads south to the old priory complex, an unrivalled group of substantially intact Medieval buildings. Beside the priory is a copious spring which supplies the island with fresh water, and is presumably the well into which the first Abbot fell and drowned after an all-night drinking binge. The priory was built on the usual plan, with the main buildings grouped around a cloister, but on a vastly reduced scale whih gives the site a unique charm. The church of St Illtud occupies the south end of the cloister, and has a small tower with a dramatically leaning spire. The dimly-lit interior of the building, with its restored timberwork and rugged stone-vaulted sanctuary, is a remarkable and atmospheric place. Against the south wall is a tall stone with a 9th-cetury Latin and Ogham inscription. The latter reads *'Maglia Dubracunas'*, while the long-winded Latin inscription and has been translated as: *'As the sign of the Cross [which] I have fashioned upon that [stone] I ask all who walk there that they pray for the soul of Catuoconus'*.

Of the ancient buildings there remains but to mention the church of St David, built in the 12th or

13th century to serve the needs of the small island community. The church is an austere, tastefully restored building, with a plain chancel, nave and west porch; a modern sacristy had been added on the north side.

Visitors approaching or leaving Caldey should notice a group of ruined buildings on St Margaret's isle, off the westernmost tip of the island. Two round chimneys can be seen on the northern building, which was originally a late-Medieval house comprising three wings set around a small courtyard. Although claimed to be the ruins of a chapel or cell, this is clearly a domestic building which was adapted and used as quarrymen's cottages in the last century. The remaining buildings on the island also date for this period of industrial activity.

LYDSTEP 'PALACE' (95)

Most people go to Lydstep to stay at the Haven caravan park, or to view the spectacular coastal scenery and the famous caves, but Lydstep has other attractions apart from picture-postcard scenery. Next to the post office stands the ivy-covered shell of the 'Old Palace', one of many derelict Medieval first-floor halls in this part of west Wales. The large hall was subdivided into a smaller parlour, with a projecting garderobe turret at one end of the building. The basement is divided into two unequally sized chambers with vaulted roofs set at right angles to each other. When the antiquarian E. T. Barnwell made a study of this building in 1867, the parlour was thatched over, and was presumably still inhabited. Barnwell also recorded another Medieval hall on the opposite side of the road, which no longer exists. Yet another old house lies a short distance away towards Tenby at Whitewell, although the remains are less intact and obscured by surrounding woodland.

MANORBIER (96)

The coastal village and castle of Manorbier received fullsome praise from the renowned 12th-century cleric and chronicler, Gerald of Wales; 'In all the broad lands of Wales, Manorbier is the most pleasant place by far'. Gerald himself was born here c. 1146, the fourth son of William de Barri and Angharad, grandaughter of the Welsh ruler Rhys ap Tewdwr. Gerald begs his reader's forgiveness for his enthusiastic description of his birthplace which, apart from a certain bias, still holds true today. The 'fortified mansion' or castle he referred to stands on a hill between two stream valleys. On the adjacent slopes were orchards, vineyards and groves of lofty hazel trees, and one of the streams was dammed to form a mill and fish-pond. The ruins of a post-Medieval mill below the castle probably occupies the site of Gerald's 12th-century mill. Along a path beyond the mill is a pepperpot-shaped dovecote, another relic of the manorial food supply.

The castle Gerald knew eight centuries ago was a comparatively simple stockade with a crude tower guarding the gate at one end, and a two-storey hall block at the other side of the courtyard. This austere and gloomy hall is the earliest stone building surviving at any castle site in west Wales and was probably built in the 1140s. Later members of the De Barri family greatly extended the castle in the 13th century; the hall and gate tower were linked by curtain walls with flanking towers, a vaulted chapel wing was added to the hall, and a new gatehouse constructed. The large outer ward on the north-east side was also enclosed with masonry walls and towers. In the later Middle Ages Manorbier was leased to a variety of owners who evidently cared little for its upkeep; by 1618 it was described as an *old ruinous castle quite decayed*. The Civil War brought the castle back out of retirement for a brief use as a Royalist stronghold, and then in the 19th century a house was built within the courtyard and the crumbling masonry repaired.

Across the valley stands the large, multi-period church of St James The Great. Young Gerald fled to this church for safety in 1153 during a Welsh attack on Tenby, and it is possible that the nave incorporates the fabric of that 12th-century building. During the 13th and 14th centuries the church was greatly enlarged and modified with the addition of a south and north aisle, a tower, and a north transept. An arched recess in the chancel contains a fine stone effigy of a proverbial 'knight in shining armour', a 14th-century member of the De Barri family. On the hillside above the church are the ruins of what may have been a monastic grange, or farm, established around 1271 when the church was granted to Monkton Priory (101). The remains of a blocked mural stair can be seen, and the ivy-covered walls of a small barn.

One more site needs to be mentioned here,

Manorbier; reconstruction of the Norman keep. Below: 19th century etching of the inner ward.

King's Quoit burial chamber, a Neolithic tomb that was constructed millenia before there was any castle or church at Manorbier. The tomb lies beside the coast path to Old Castle Head, and the large flat capstone is supported by three low slabs. No trace remains of a surrounding cairn which, owing to the location, could never have been very extensive, and probably consisted of loose stones heaped against the sides of the chamber.

HODGESTON CHURCH (97)

Hodgeston is a typical example of a south Pembrokeshire church, with a vaulted nave, chancel and a lofty slender tower rising to a corbelled parapet. It is also in a very accessible location, only a few yards from the A4139 between Manorbier and Pembroke. This 13th-century building was modified in the 14th century when the chancel was rebuilt, possibly at the instigation of Bishop Gower of St David's. A magnificent triple sedilia and piscina in the Decorated style is a legacy of this work.

On marshy ground bordering the church is the side of a moated manor house. Vegetation has covered the earthworks, but the general plan is still visible — a raised platform 60 feet-square with a surrounding wet ditch. Fenton wrote that there was a ruined 'religious house' here in the 18th century, and this might suggest that the moat was a parsonage or rector's dwelling. As late as 1870 the remains of a small building could be seen on the platform.

LAMPHEY BISHOP'S PALACE (98)

The Bishop's Palace at Lamphey is only slightly less magnificent than its counterpart at St David's (147), and both palatial residences remain as visible symbols of the wealth and prestige of the Medieval Church. Here at Lamphey there were gardens, orchards, fish-ponds and a deer park; a place where the Bishop could relax and live like a rich country magnate, indulging in a lifestyle that would have had the body of the Cathedral's founder turning in his grave. Although we have documentary evidence to imply the existence of some kind of dwelling here as far back as the late 11th century, all the existing buildings are no earlier than the 13th century.

Visitors approach the palace through the outer courtyard wall, to where a solitary gatetower marks the entrance to the vanished inner court.

The parapet of the tower is carried on a series of decorative arches, an architectural trademark of that great building Bishop, Henry de Gower (1328-47), to be seen also at the St David's Palace. The buildings beyond the gatehouse include a modest early 13th-century hall, a more ornate 'Camera' (i.e. the Bishop's private chamber), and an early 16th-century chapel with elaborate traceried windows. This late addition was the work of Bishop Edward Vaughan. Beyond the main block stands Bishop Gower's Great Hall, a first-floor hall with a vaulted basement. From the hall a stair leads up to the battlements, where a good view of the whole complex is obtained. At the Dissolution the estate was surrendered to the Crown and later granted to Richard Devereux, Earl of Essex. Although an attempt was made to convert the ornate, but cumbersome Medieval buildings to Elizabethan use, the Palace was soon abandoned and left to decay. The site is now cared for by CADW: Welsh Historic Monuments.

Across the valley in the modern village stands the much restored parish church, dedicated to St Tyfai, a nephew of St Teilo. The Medieval cruciform church has been extensively restored twice in the 19th century, apart from the battlemented tower. Opposite the gate is a large slab embedded in a garden wall, formerly inscribed with a cross, but nothing can now be seen on the rough surface. A short distance away beside the Ridgeway road to Penally is a prominent 'Flemish' chimney, now standing in monolithic isolation, having outlived the house for which it was built.

CAREW (99)

Magnificent Carew castle is one of the few sites in west Wales where visitors can see the various changes and modifications which occurred with a feudal stronghold in almost continous occupation. This particular castle has been abandoned for the last 300 years or so, but it nevertheless encapsulates the changes in defensive and domestic architecture which afflicted the evolution of the Medieval castle.

The site was occupied long before the Normans arrived; continuing excavations have uncovered finds of Romano-British date, and a series of rock-cut ditches underlying the later stone castle. Gerald of Windsor, castellan of Pembroke, is reputed to have founded Carew at the beginning of the 12th

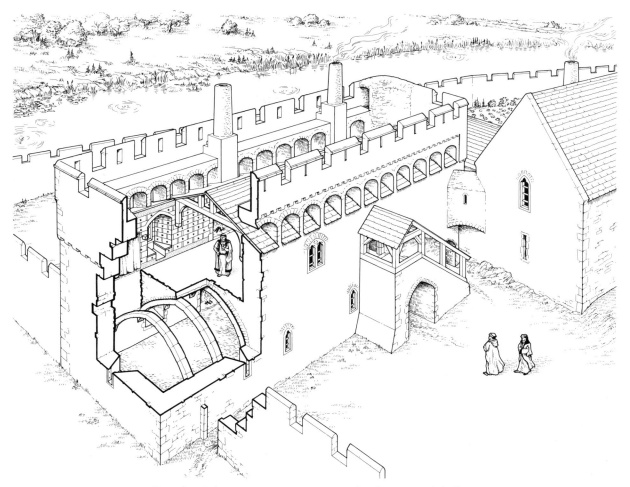

Lamphey Palace; cutaway reconstruction of Bishop Gower's hall.

century. Nothing survives above ground of that early stronghold, but archaeologists have recently discovered a Norman bread oven and a silver penny of King Stephen (1135-54). Until the late 13th century, Carew was a relatively unsophisticated castle defended by timber palisades and earth-works. A small stone gatetower was built c. 1200, but it was up to Sir Nicholas de Carew (d. 1311) to initiate the rebuilding of his ancestral stronghold. Sir Nicholas constructed a large polygonal en-closure (the present inner ward) bristling with defensive towers of various shapes — round, square, hexagonal and D-shaped. The Great Hall stood between the two large western towers, while the Lesser Hall and Chapel Tower lay on the opposite side of the courtyard. A larger outer ward occupied the ridge to the east.

In 1480 Sir Edmund Carew mortgaged his family home to the illustrious Sir Rhys ap Thomas, who embarked on a refurbishing scheme which included the removal of the castle's more military features. Narrow loop-holes and gloomy Medieval win-dows were opened out to let light flood into the banqueting hall and the many lavish residential chambers. To the Great Hall Sir Rhys added an imposing storied porch with heraldic decorations, and a large oriel window and minstrel's gallery, from where musicians could entertain the guests assembled in the hall below. Much finely-decorated stonework survives to indicate Sir Rhys' ambitious aesthetic tastes.

Less than a century was to pass before Carew was further modified and transformed into an elegant Elizabethan country house, by the flam-

Carew Castle.

boyant Sir John Perrot (see 117). Perrot was granted governorship of Carew during the reign of Queen Mary, and in the late 1580s he began work on a new range of buildings on the north side of the castle. Seen from across the river, Perrot's wing forms the most striking part of the castle, a three-storey block with rows of tall mullioned windows, projecting oriel turrets and sham battlements. It is not known for certain if the building was ever finished, for an inventory drawn up in 1592 before his death mentions a locked room containing 'so much glasse ready to be sett upp as will grace all the windowes of ye newe buildinge'.

The castle-cum-mansion continued to be occupied by tenant owners, but the building was in decay, and its downfall was hastened by its use as a Royalist stronghold in the Civil War. In 1644 the castle was surrendered to the Parliamentarian army, and then partially demolished. Part of the Medieval village was also razed to provide a clear field of fire, although a large round chimney (minus its house) survives in the grounds of the 'Flemish Tea Gardens'. The Castle is now cared for

by the Pembrokeshire National Coast Park Authority, and is open to the public from Easter to October. Parts of the site are inaccessible while excavation and consolidation work is in progress.

The village of Carew is not only graced with an impressive ruined fortress, but also a magnificent 11th-century memorial cross covered with inter-lacing patterns. A Latin panel on the back of this 14 foot-high cross commemorates Maredudd ap Edwin, joint ruler of west Wales, who was killed in battle in 1035. This ranks with the crosses at Nevern (61) and Penally (93) as the finest Dark Age sculptured stone in Wales.

Carew Cheriton Church

The parish church of St John the Baptist is an imposing edifice of 14th-15th century date, domin-ated by a lofty, buttressed tower of Somerset type. The church lies about half a mile south of the great fortress, just off a road leading to the Old Rectory antiques centre. The interior of the church is initially disappointing, with drab roughcast walls and peeling plaster, but the brightly-lit chancel

Carew Cheriton; cutaway view of the mortuary chapel. In plan the chapel is identical to many vaulted domestic buildings in west Wales.

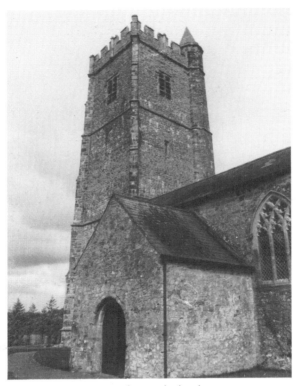

Carew; the parish church.

with its heraldic floor tiles of c. 1500 is a delight. Some of the tiles are decorated with the three raven crest of Sir Rhys ap Thomas, and are reputed to have been brought here from the castle chapel. Three effigies fill niches in the chancel walls; beside the triple sedilia is a tiny effigy of a young girl, feet resting on a dog and her head sheltered by angels. Both effigy and sedilia were only discovered in 1843 when an accumulated layer of plaster was removed. On the opposite side is a damaged effigy of a priest, but more impressive is the neighbouring sculpture of Sir Nicholas de Carew (d. 1311), the builder of much of the nearby castle. The unknown stonecarver has imbued this fine monument with a lifelike and vibrant quality unmarked in the other effigies; the body is twisted towards the spectator, right hand drawing a sword, as if Sir Nicholas is in the act of leaping off the cold slab to defend once more the Carew lands from any trespasser. Even this worthy knight could not have deflected the unpredictable Welsh weather when, in 1926, the 15th-century tower was struck by lightning, costing almost £2000 to repair.

The north transept contains two pompous 17th-century tomb-effigies of Sir John Carew (d. 1637) and his wife Elizabeth; the former wears ceremonial armour of the period, providing an interesting contrast with the more primitive tin suit of his ancestor in the chancel.

In the churchyard stands a 15th-century mortuary chapel, which has been used as a school-room since at least 1625. While the children were taught basic lessons in the first-floor chapel, human bones were stored in the vaulted charnel house beneath. In the chapel can be seen a partially blocked-up traceried window, and a finely decorated piscina where the sacramental vessels were washed. Apart from these ecclesiastical details, the chapel differs little from other Medieval vaulted buildings in this part of Wales.

One final site of historic interest here is the nearby Rectory, a three-storey tower house incorporated into a post-Medieval mansion. When Fenton visited it much of the building was in ruins, but it has since been restored. The tower itself resembled that at Haroldston (117), for it also functioned as a gatehouse, and the blocked entrance arch can be seen in the north wall.

UPTON (100)

Upton Castle is a private residence and is, unfortunately, not open to the public, but the surrounding grounds and restored Medieval chapel can be visited during the summer months. The estate lies on the banks of the Cleddau, about two miles north-west of Carew, and can be reached along a minor road from Milton to Carew. Upton is not a true castle, but a 14th or 15th-century first-floor hall, built in the form of a fortified gatehouse. The main block comprises a hall between two round turrets, with an adjoining vaulted gate passage and a round tower. Further additions in the 16th, 17th and 19th centuries have greatly altered and extended the building.

The nearby chapel was the private mausoleum of the Lords of Upton, the Malefant family, and the building contains a remarkable collection of Medieval tomb-effigies. There are four, and the most impressive is the armoured figure of Sir William Malefant (d. 1362), set in a richly decorated canopied recess in the north wall. A marginally less splendid effigy of his wife can be seen in the chancel. Visitors should also note a diminutive candle-holder, in the form of a clenched fist, protruding from the wall beside the chancel arch.

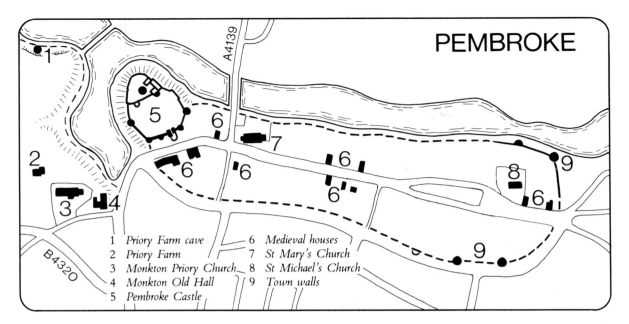

PEMBROKE (101)

In a remote period at least 10,000 years ago, a small group of nomadic hunters sheltered in a cave in the limestone cliffs bordering a river valley. These people, known to us only by the discovery of their primitive flint implements, are the earliest inhabitants of Pembroke. Thousands of years later in the Bronze Age, the same cave was occupied briefly by an itinerant craftsman, for three tools of the new and highly-prized metal have also been found by modern archaeologists. The skeletal remains of at least 3 individuals suggests that this dark, subterranean shelter was later used as a burial site. A few millenia passed before a more determined effort was made to colonize the district. In AD 1093 the Normans arrived here and built an earth and timber castle to enforce and defend their hold on their surrounding land. The invaders chose a naturally defended headland site above the river, and drew a bank and ditch across the narrow neck of the ridge. This 'slender fortress of turf and stakes', as it was later described, successfully endured a Welsh uprising in 1094, when the resourceful Normans fooled the besieging army into believing that the castle was well armed and fully provisioned, and could endure a prolonged siege. This so disheartened the Welsh that they gave up and went home.

The site chosen for that early castle was an admirable one for defence — the rocky tip of a long, sinuous ridge, sandwiched between a marshy stream on the south, and the Pembroke river on the north. This restricted area nevertheless dictated the unique layout of the adjoining town, a single long street flanked by houses and narrow burgage plots. During the 12th and 13th centuries the settlement flourished, and the castle and town defences were gradually refortified in stone. The spiritual needs of the townspeople were served by two parish churches within the walls, St Michael's and St Mary's; only the latter however, retains any early masonry. A Benedictine Priory was also established c. 1098 on the hillside across from the castle.

The relative affluence of the Medieval borough is reflected by the survival of a large number of early domestic buildings, such as the cottages at East Gate, and a small tower house behind the York Inn. Many other modern houses incorporate vaulted cellars belonging to their Medieval precursors. By far the most impressive domestic building is **Monkton Old Hall**, beside the Priory church. Although heavily restored, this private dwelling retains many early features, including a prominent round chimney and a rib-vaulted undercroft. The nearby **Priory Farm** is a less obvious Medieval building, but the remains of a corbelled parapet survives of this former tower house. However, the most dominant survivor of the Middle Ages is Pembroke's mighty castle, one of the largest and most powerful in Wales.

Pembroke; cutaway view of Monkton Old Hall.

The castle was founded by Roger of Montgomery in 1093, but the existing stone fortress was not built until the end of the 12th century by the Earl of Pembroke, William Marshal. Marshal was one of the greatest knights of the Middle Ages, and he and his sons used the castle as a fortified base and embarkation point for the Norman conquests in Ireland. Marshal rebuilt the old timber defences in stone, embodying all the latest military innovations that foreshadowed the development of castle architecture for the next half century. The large outer ward was provided with a thick enclosing wall studded with round towers, a strong gatehouse and a barbican. The more secure inner ward contained the main domestic buildings, including a hall, chapel and kitchen, all overshadowed by the great bulk of the keep. This is Pembroke's crowning glory, a massive, four-storey round tower 75 feet-high, roofed over with a stone dome and triple wall-walks. The echoing, cavernous interior is even more impressive today,

lacking its timber floors. Most of the surviving masonry of the castle belongs to the period of the Earl Marshal, c. 1190-1219, although later owners improved the somewhat spartan accommodation.

It was at Pembroke castle that the future king Henry VII was born in 1457, and when John Leland later visited the decaying fortress around 1540, he was shown 'the Chaumbre wher King Henri the VII was borne' and a newly-made fireplace bearing the royal arms, in memory of that event. Pembroke was the only town in west Wales to declare for Parliament in the Civil War, but in 1648 the garrison changed sides, and Cromwell ordered an assault on the castle. The damage done by Roundhead cannonfire was repaired in 1880-3, when much of the ruinous castle was restored.

The most unexpected feature of Pembroke is the great cave underneath the Northern Hall, reached from the clifftop via a narrow winding stair. The north facing entrance was partially sealed up when the cave was used as a boat-house in the Middle

Ages. Pembroke's second cave lies 400 yards west of the castle, in a disused quarry above the riverside path. This is **Cathole**, or Priory Farm Cave, a single, low tunnel penetrating the limestone cliff for about 100 feet. When discovered and excavated in 1906-7, the accumulated debris had so filled up the cave that it was impossible to explore for more than 30 feet. The finds included flints of Late Upper Palaeolithic date, Bronze Age implements and 14th-15th century potsherds. A large quantity of Ice Age animal bones were also found, including those of reindeer, bear and mammoth, all gnawed by carnivorous tenants, when the cave was used as a hyaena den.

Monkton Priory Church was, like the castle, founded in the late 11th century, although the existing building is much later in date. The long vaulted nave probably incorporates masonry of late 12th-13th-century date, and may have served the needs of the monastic community, before the chancel was added later. At the Dissolution the nave remained in parochial use while the chancel was unroofed and left to decay; it was up to the Victorians to restore the chancel to its former glory. The interior of the church is stately and spacious, and the lofty nave draws the eye towards the beautifully restored east end. An intra-mural stair beside the main door led up to a former room above the porch. The vaulted south transept forms the ground floor of the tower. and it contains an imposing altar-tomb to Sir Francis Meyrick (d. 1603). Other equally impressive wall tablets can be seen in the nave, commemorating the Owens of Orielton. From the churchyard a good view can be obtained of the adjacent Medieval hall, and the walls and towers of the fortified borough.

DRY BURROWS TUMULI (102)

This impressive group of Bronze Age burial mounds lies beside the B4320 near the Speculation Inn, 1½ miles south-west of Pembroke. There are no less than seven earthen barrows here, four of

Pembroke; the approach to the castle gatehouse.

which are particularly prominent and can be seen from the roadside. Richard Fenton was evidently impressed with the remains at Dry Burrows: 'the largest group I ever recollect to have seen in this county' he wrote. In a rare moment of restraint, Fenton commented that an excavation of the barrows would be 'too great an undertaking for a private individual', but this did not deter his son, from digging into some of the mounds, and uncovering the remains of four cremation burials.

About ¾ mile further west there is another roadside mound, Corston Beacon. This low, grass-covered mound was more carefully excavated in 1927, when it was found to consist of a bowl-shaped cairn with a central burial cist. Underneath the two-ton capstone lay the skeleton of a 'Beaker' man, who had died here around 1600 BC. Beside the skeleton was a small bronze dagger, a prized possession to be used in the afterlife. The whole of this area was evidently of some importance to the Bronze Age settlers of south Pembrokeshire, for another barrow group lies further along the ridge at Wallaston Green, beside the Pwllchrochan road.

PWLLCHROCHAN (103)

Pwllchrochan used to be a beautiful place before the advent of modern industry. Now this remote and secluded 14th-century church is sandwiched between the Texaco oil refinery and the Pembroke power station. But the view to the north is still the same (probably unchanged since the Middle Ages), a narrow wooded dingle leading down to the haven, with the church tucked into the hillside. Most of the existing structure was raised 'In the year of our Lord, 1342', as a mural tablet inscribed with Lombardic capitals informs us. This was the work of Ralph Beneger, rector of Pwllchrochan, who lies interred in the nave beneath a slab bearing his effigy. A weathered inscription along the edge of his tomb reads 'HIC IACIT RADULPHUS BENEGER'. The chancel is linked by a passage-squint to the north transept, while the vaulted south transept forms the ground floor of a two-storey tower, topped with a diminutive spire. Pwllchrochan church was restored in the 19th century, and more work may follow, for this forlorn building is now derelict and empty, awaiting further restoration.

RHOSCROWTHER (104)

This is a more fortunate church than Pwllchrochan, for not only does it lie in a more populous part of the countryside (and is therefore not so run-down), but it is situated in a valley away from the prosaic sights and smells of the Texaco refinery.

The church is a pre-Norman foundation, probably established by St Deguman who was born in west Wales and in later life sailed across to Somerset to carry on the good work. There is a holy well in the marshy dingle to the south, dedicated to this saint, and a small chapel adjoining the nave of the parish church is claimed to be the saint's oratory or cell. However, the present building is the result of centuries of modification and enlargement. The earliest masonry is probably the nave and chancel, extended in the 14th century by the addition of two transepts, a tower, and a south chapel. The tower was built above the vaulted south transept and has two vaulted upper floors, perhaps designed to support the weight of a spire. None was ever built, and the usual battlemented parapet is enlivened by little pinnacles at the four corners. The south chapel contains an impressive 14th-century effigy of a lady, and above the door of the modern porch are two stone heraldic plaques, said to have been brought from Angle church (106).

Rhoscrowther; the parish church.

Eastington; cutaway view of the tower house.

Two examples of early domestic architecture need to be highlighted here: opposite the church stands Hilton Farm, probably of 16th or 17th-century date. A tall and massive chimney is a particularly prominent feature. Of greater importance is nearby Eastington, a late Medieval first-floor hall, now a private residence on the edge of the refinery. A public footpath leads past the outside. This was another dwelling of the large and influential Perrot family, and the building shares many features in common with other Medieval houses already mentioned, particularly the Old Palace at Lydstep (95). There is a vaulted undercroft, a large hall on the upper floor approached by an outside stair, and a projecting garderobe turret. But at Eastington the presence of a battlemented parapet and wall-walk indicated that defence, as much as domestic comfort, was uppermost in the architect's mind.

DEVIL'S QUOIT AND KILPAISON BARROW (105)

The Devil's Quoit on Kilpaison Burrows is the only one of several similarly named monuments in this area to be a genuine 'quoit', i.e. a burial chamber. The remains are unfortunately not very impressive, and lie beside the B4319 Angle to Castlemartin road. Further east along the same ridge is the site of Kilpaison barrow, an Early Bronze Age burial mound. Excavation in 1925 revealed it to have been a complex site which had been used for burial on several occasions. The first inhumation was the cremated remains of a young lady, placed in a pit before a miniature standing stone. This was then covered over with an earthen mound about 4 feet high and at least 50 feet across. At a later date in the Bronze Age, five secondary cremation burials were inserted into the mound. Finally, a slab-lined 'coffin' orientated east to west was constructed, and the body of a 30-year-old man placed inside. The orientation and slab-lined grave are features indicative of an Early Christian burial; if so then the undertaker showed no reluctance at using an earlier 'pagan' sepulchral mound.

ANGLE (106)

Angle is a straggling village at the furthest tip of south Pembrokeshire, a pleasing mixture of old and new. The rugged stonework of Medieval buildings peer from between the brightly painted walls of more recent dwellings. The place-name may derive from *ongull*, the Norse word for fiord, or, as Richard Fenton put it *'from being . . . in angulo, in a nook'*; both are equally appropriate and it is up to the visitor to choose. The parish church of St Mary consists of a nave, chancel and tower, but has been extensively restored. Of greater interest is the little fisherman's chapel in the graveyard, a vaulted building similar to the detached chapel at Carew (99). A priest's effigy, which Fenton saw in the churchyard *'almost covered with the sward, and much effaced'*, has been removed for safe keeping to the first-floor chapel. The vault beneath was formerly used as a charnel house.

Directly opposite the church is a prominent, Scottish-style 15th-century tower house, once part of a larger fortified manor belonging to the Sherborne family. The interior of the building is divided up into four small chamber linked by a newel stair. The original entrance was on the first floor and reached across a drawbridge for added security. The tower is now a gutted shell, but when the floors and roof were in place, and the tiny windows secured with wooden shutters, the whole must have been intolerably gloomy and cramped. A short distance uphill is a large dovecot, a handy store of fresh meat in times of scarcity.

Behind the village post office is another ruined building more characteristic of Medieval Scotland than Wales. This two-storied block has been labelled as a 'nunnery' or 'almshouse', but it is clearly a semi-fortified domestic building with a first-floor hall above a storeroom (there was a timber floor rather than the more usual vaulted undercroft).

EAST BLOCKHOUSE (107)

Leaving Angle for the furthermost tip of the peninsula, the visitor soon reaches East Blockhouse point overlooking the entrance to Milford Haven, 'one of the fairest harbours of this realm' s a Tudor historian put it. The defence of this great inland waterway was of considerable importance in earlier times — there are Iron Age forts and Medieval castles along the many inlets and rivers, and in the late 19th century Lord Palmerston ordered the building of numerous forts to guard the Haven against possible French attack. Palmerston's xenophobic constructions still survive in brooding decay, but this was merely the completion of a scheme envisaged by an even earlier government of over four centuries ago. In the reign of Henry VIII two 'blockhouses', or artillery forts, were built to guard the Haven against an envisaged Spanish/French invasion. They were never completed and were, in any case, ineffectively sited. Further defensive plans were drawn up in the 1580s during the Armada crisis, but these, too, were never carried out. Of West Blockhouse, Dale, only its 19th-century successor remains, but fragments of the Angle blockhouse have managed to survive on the very edge of the cliff, a stones' throw from fortifications of 19th and 20th-century date. It was originally built in the form of a round tower with artillery loop-holes, and an etching of 1881 shows that it had a corbelled parapet. Although the surviving remains are not very impressive, this is the only Welsh example of the 16th-century forts seen elsewhere in England at Deal, Pendennis, Camber and Sandown.

Less than one mile further east is a far older coastal fortification, an Iron Age defended settlement at *Sheep Island* promontory. The island itself has traces of rectangular huts (see also 127), while the headland was defended by a single rampart, since damaged by the construction of a World War I look-out tower. Incredible as it may seem, there was an earlier watch tower here, possibly of Medieval or Tudor date. Only a few fragments survive of this, but the 16th-century historian, George Owen, reported seeing 'the remnant of a tower built upon the entrance' to the headland fort. Few other sites in west Wales have been so variously defended against different enemies through the centuries.

CASTLEMARTIN (108)

Castlemartin lies on the doorstep of the Royal Armoured Corps Firing Range, almost 6000 acres of land incorporating some of the most spectacular coastal scenery in Wales, and a scattering of arch-aeological sites. The straggling village lies along a ridgeway route, 4½ miles south-west of Pembroke. At one end there is an 18th-century cattle pound which, in its time, has been used as an air-raid shelter, a gun emplacement and a roundabout. At the rear of the post office can be seen the earth-works of the castle of Castlemartin. This was pres-umably the headquarters of the Norman lord of the district, although the remains are more reminiscent of an Iron Age hillfort.

There was a burial ground here long before the Normans arrived, for a cross stone of 7th-9th century date is kept inside the Medieval parish church. This well-kept building is dedicated to St. Michael, and lies in a hollow below the village, away from the prevailing winds. Like many other churches, that at Castlemartin has undergone con-siderable rebuilding and extension, but remarkably the process has also been reversed, for the church has 'shrunk' to its present form. Blocked doors and arches indicate the former existence of two side chapels, a north transept and a west porch. An obvious break in the masonry of the tower indi-cates that the present parapet is an addition, and that the tower was originally finished off with a gabled 'saddleback' — a rare feature in Pembroke-shire churches.

On the hill above the church stands the 'old rectory', an outwardly unexciting building, but containing a unique series of internal stone arches. In the 18th century a kitchen was added at one end, but the rest of the building is puzzling and defies interpretation; was it a small chapel converted into a cottage? a dwelling built of materials brought from the church? or is it simply a post-Medieval folly?

FLIMSTON (109)

Flimston chapel is a sad, forlorn building way out on the bleak expanse of the Castlemartin firing range. Access is only possible at certain times of the week when the range is not in use, and the coast road is open. The building is a larger and much restored version of the better known chapel at nearby St Govans (110), consisting of a single vaulted chamber, possibly of 15th-century origin.

From the churchyard look west across the range to the shattered hulks of old farmhouses, some dating back to the Middle Ages and all deserted on

the setting up of the range. On the skyline can be seen the tall chimneys of Pricaston, a 16th-century mansion engulfed by outbuildings and additions of later years. Closer at hand is Flimston Farm, a large rambling complex, roofless except for the house. The spacious windows and liberal use of brick suggests an 18th or 19th-century date, but the north end of the range encapsulates a Medieval first-floor hall, with a familiar round chimney and a vaulted undercroft. Flimston is currently inaccessible, although plans are in hand for its preservation and further public access.

Beyond the chapel the coast road ends in a cliff-top car park overlooking the magnificent rock formations of the Green Bridge and Eligug Stacks. When the range is not in use a public footpath can be followed eastwards to St Govans, passing three examples of Iron Age promontory forts, at the Devil's Punchbowl, Bullslaughter Bay and Buckspool Down.

ST GOVAN'S CHAPEL (110)

Perhaps nowhere else is Wales is the 'Age of the Saints' so eloquently evoked than at St Govan's chapel, and the lack of historical documentation relating to this site is more than adequately made up for by legend and folk-lore. The identity of Govan has long been a puzzler; Gobhan, the Irish Abbot of Dairinis Monastery, Wexford, is a bettter candidate than Gawain of the Green Knight fame. Regardless of its traditional Dark Age origin, the existing building is unlikely to be earlier than the 13th century. St Govan's lies at the end of the coast road from Bosherston, about six miles south of Pembroke, and is accessible only when the adjacent firing range is not in use. From the inevit-able cliff-top car park a long flight of steps leads down to the chapel which lies wedged in a narrow coastal valley, almost as if it had grown out of the surrounding rugged cliffs. The interior is dark and mysterious, and overhead there is a pointed stone vault. A door beside the altar leads into a narrow rock cervice that, legend has it, opened to shelter and hide the persecuted saint, whose rib marks can be seen on the rock. A little spring beside the entrance is said never to flow over the chapel floor, and the 'healing' waters were scooped out and drunk from a limpet shell. Another well (now dry) lies below the chapel, and was used for curing rheumatism, failing eyesight and lameness. Those cured left their crutches behind on the altar as a votive offering and proof of the water's curative powers.

BOSHERSTON CHURCH (111)

Bosherston is renowned more for its magnificent lily ponds than as a historic site, but there is the venerable parish church of St Michael and all Angels, and many 17th century houses in the area which can be identified by their massive chimney stacks. The church lies on a hill overlooking the lakes which were formed in the 18th century as part of the neighbouring Stackpole Estate. A car park beside the church allows for easy access to the many waymarked footpaths hereabouts.

St Michael's church is an impressive cruciform building of 13th-14th century origin, with a vaulted nave and twin transepts and a later tower at the west end. The chancel vault was replaced by a timber roof in the 19th century. In the north transept there is an elegant 14th-century effigy of a lady, the head covered by a decorated canopy and the feet resting on a greyhound. An earlier and less intact effigy can be seen in the opposite transept. A 14th-century preaching cross in the churchyard is a rare survivor, and should not be missed.

STACKPOLE WARREN (112)

Evidence for the agricultural and religious activities of ancient Man can be found in abundance on the expanse of Stackpole Warren, although the remains must be carefully sought out. The above-ground features include field walls, enclosures and settlement sites, but more impressive is the Devil's Quoit standing stone. This 7 feet-high monolith was the subject of a fascinating excavation by the Dyfed Archaeological Trust, which revealed that the stone was only one part of a ritual complex hidden and preserved by blown sand. The site was first occupied by an Early Bronze Age round hut, which survived only as a series of gulleys and post-holes (marking the former positions of upright timbers supporting a peaked roof). Some time after the hut had been burnt down, the site was partly overlain by a remarkable bullet-shaped arrangement of over 3000 small upright stones, in effect, a megalithic pin-cushion. Then the stone itself was set up, along with a wooden post (a totem pole?), within the area

of the smaller stone setting. A long period elapsed when the site was abandoned and partly covered by soil and sand, but its former significance was not forgotten. During the Iron Age and Roman period several burials took place here, and finally the monument's use ended (as it had begun) as a settlement site.

There are two fine Iron Age promontory forts in the vicinity worth visiting. The nearest is **Fishponds Camp** on a ridge above the Stackpole lakes The discovery of a bronze pin of early Iron Age type suggests that a small settlement was established here by early Celtic immigrants. The weak, inner rampart may have formed part of that camp, with additional defences added later in the Iron Age. Further along the coast towards Manorbier is **Greenala Point fort** a very impressive multivallate site which is also likely to be a two-period site. Much of the interior has been lost through erosion, but the outer defences survive.

STACKPOLE (113)

If we are to believe Gerald of Wales, twelfth-century Pembrokeshire was a particularly troublesome place to live in, as two landowners found to their cost when poltergeists invaded their homes, scattered rubbish about and tore people's clothes. Worse still, the spirits had an annoying habit of embarrassing people by talking openly about their darkest secrets and misdeeds. At Stackpole Court, Sir Elidyr de Stackpole had a most efficient steward who provided anything the family needed, and always turned up promptly for work. This red-haired youth was the offspring of a demonic incubus, and when his origin was revealed, he was promptly fired from his post. Evidently equal opportunities for incubi did not exist in Medieval Wales!

The church in which the Stackpoles worshipped (and where the steward never ventured) still stands, but alas the ancestral mansion is no more, having been demolished in 1962. The existing chrch of Saints James and Elidyr is a large and imposing structure of 13th-14th century date, set at the head of a wooded valley 2¼ miles south of Pembroke. The early chancel and nave was greatly extended by the addition of two vaulted transepts, a tall, narrow tower, and a rib-vaulted south chapel. There is a remarkable collection of carved stone monuments inside, many associated with the own-

Devil's Quoit; an imaginary reconstruction of the standing stone complex as it may have appeared in the Bronze Age.

ers of the neighbouring estate. There are two 14th-century female effigies in the south chapel, along with a characteristic early 17th-century monument to Roger and Abertha Lort, complete with painted effigies of the interred worthies, and miniature figures of their twelve children.

An earlier, and more impressive monument lies within a richly decorated niche in the chancel: the armoured figure of Sir Richard de Stackpole, last of that line. Along the front of this mid-14th century tomb are panels depicting huntsmen, soldiers and wimpled women. Not to be outdone, Sir Richard's wife, Margaret Turberville of Coity, was provided with an equally impressive monument. On one side of this slab-like altar tomb are richly-carved flowered panels, with grimacing faces and weeping figures. Lady Margaret lies full length with hands folded neatly in prayer, feet resting on two dogs guarded by angels.

There is one other monument worth highlighting in this church of superlative monuments; a 5th or early 6th-century inscribed stone commem-orating 'Camulorix, son of Fannucus'. Unlike the Stackpole effigies where the Medieval mason has carved the idealized likenesses of the local land-owners, this Dark Age stone had only a simple inscription to commemorate this otherwise unknown princeling who died here over 14 centuries ago.

ST PETROX (114)

This is one of three tall churches which form conspicuous landmarks for miles around. The others are St Twynell's and Warren, the latter now an empty shell awaiting restoration. St Petrox is perhaps the most impressive of the three, and it is certainly the most accessible, lying on a breezy hilltop beside the B4319 to Pembroke. The chancel is modern, but it contains a 17th-century brass memorial to William Lloyd, rector of the parish. Another memorial commemmorates Jane Mansell of Muddlescwm, whose headless ghost is said to ride around the countryside in a carriage driven by a headless coachman, and drawn by a headless horse!

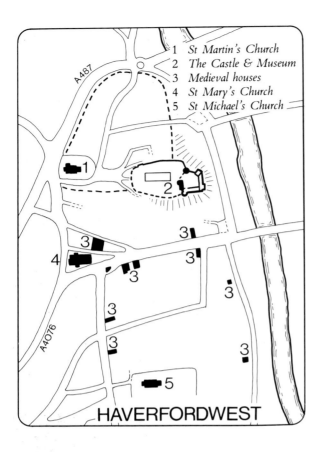

1	St Martin's Church
2	The Castle & Museum
3	Medieval houses
4	St Mary's Church
5	St Michael's Church

HAVERFORDWEST

Haverfordwest and The Milford Peninsula

(Sites 115–128)

Haverfordwest (115)

Haverfordwest has long outgrown the boundaries of the original Medieval settlement, established in the shadow of an early 12th-century castle. This castle was founded by Gilbert de Clare, Earl of Pembroke, around 1110. For the site of his stronghold Earl Gilbert chose a steep-sided ridge overlooking the highest tidal point of the Cleddau river — a good strategic location, for not only did it overlook an early crossing place, but the castle could be reached by boat even if the overland supply routes were in enemy control.

The early settlement was known initially as 'Castleton', and lay on the ridge west and north of the castle. The defences were undoubtedly of timber, and it was not until the mid 13th century

that the simple defensive circuit was replaced by a stone wall and gates. The inhabitant's spiritual needs were served by the market-side church of St Martin's, the earliest of the town's three parish churches. Such a cramped location was not endured by the burgesses for long, and by the end of the 12th century houses had grown up around St Mary's church on the opposite side of the valley. A third church, dedicated to St Thomas the Martyr was established further to the south, just outside the limits of the Medieval town. Also beyond the town boundary stood the leper hospital of 'St Mary Mawdlins' (now Merlin's Bridge), where part of the chapel can be seen. Sometime before 1200, Robert de Haverford founded a priory of Augustinian Canons on land bordering the river a short distance south of the town. A second monastic house was later established by the Dominican 'Black' Friars in Bridge Street, below the castle. Both establishments met with the usual fate at the Dissolution, and only the shattered walls of the priory survive above ground today.

During the later Middle Ages the prosperity of the town grew, and a valuable coastal trade with Bristol developed in the 16th century — a period when Haverfordwest was described as 'the best buylt, the most civil and quickest occupied Towne in South Wales'. But plague, the silting up of the river, and the growth of Milford Haven checked further development. It was during the 17th century that the castle, which had defended the townsfolk for over five centuries (and had successfully endured three violent sieges), was finally humbled by gunpowder in the Civil War. The ultimate indignity for this ancient stronghold was for Cromwell to order the townsfolk to demolish it themselves. Ravaged by plague and hardship, the beleaguered burgesses made a half-hearted job of it, and the ruined building was subsequently converted into a prison. A later prison block in the outer ward now houses the County Museum.

Like Pembroke and Tenby, Haverfordwest has a fine collection of Medieval and post-Reformation town houses. Massive projecting chimneys proclaim a 17th-century origin for some buildings, such as the Carmarthen Arms, while Munt's Jewellers (High Street) with its lateral corbelled stack, is Medieval. The nearby No. 15 High Street contains two finely carved fireplaces, one c. 1500 and the other dated 1614. This building may have been a town house of the Perrots of Haroldston, and may be identified as the 'Great House' mentioned in a document of 1596. There are two vaulted buildings beside St Mary's church; one is now Swales Music Shop, and the other (erroneously known as 'The Old Crypt') stands on the opposite side of the road. Another domestic building of some importance stood at the rear of a cafe in Quay Street. This was a two-storey tower house of the type already described at West Tarr and Carswell (91), and it has been dismantled and moved to the Welsh Folk Museum at St Fagans in Glamorgan, where it will be re-assembled as a permanent exhibit.

The castle is undoubtedly the most impressive relic of the Medieval town, and the great cliff-like walls still dominate the shops and houses clustered about the base of the hill. The oldest surviving masonry is a late 12th-century oblong keep, set at the furthest end of the ridge. The interior has been completely gutted, but the outer wall remains, embedded into the later curtain wall which dates from c. 1289. Much of this work too has suffered from all the post-Medieval modifications, and the

entire west side, including the gatehouse, has been swept away. Two round towers survive, and the position of the Great Hall is indicated by a row of tall windows in the south wall.

Of the three parish churches of Haverfordwest the most distinguished is undoubtedly **St Mary's**, an imposing, cathedral-like edifice at the top of High Street. The core of the building was probably constructed after a Welsh raid in 1220, but much of its present appearance is due to extensive reconstruction in the 15th and 16th centuries. Before entering, visitors should take note of the exterior, particularly the stumpy tower (bereft of its steeple) and the line of the original high-pitched roof, preserved below the later clerestory. The interior is spacious and musty, with a splendid camber-beam roof with carved bosses. Faces adorn the stone corbels supporting the mian timbers. The unbridled imagination and humour of a Medieval stonecarver is seen to good effect on the capitals of the north aisle arcade: the intertwining plant, animal and human forms include a harp-playing monkey, and a drunkard sadly turning his empty

Haverfordwest; the castle.

mug upside-down. Memorials to past worthies include an effigy of an un-named Medieval pilgrim, and an ostentatious wall-tablet to John Philipps of Picton Castle (d. 1736), adorned with weeping cherubs. The church is also renowned for a surviving fragment of a late 15th-century bench end, carved with a stylized figure of St Michael slaying the dragon. This has been built into a modern stall beside the chancel arch.

South of St Mary's stands the church of St Thomas the Martyr, a 19th-century building apart from the Medieval tower. Within is a broken 14th-century graveslab carved with a cross and a man's face, 'Richard the palmer', a pilgrim of the Holy Land. The last of the churches, St Martin's, lies within the area of the original Norman settlement, just outside the castle gates. The diminutive spire is a modern addition to this 13th–14th-century building, which has been thoroughly restored.

On the riverbank south of the town stands the remains of the **Augustinian Priory** of St Mary and St Thomas the Martyr. This was founded before 1200, and work started on building the

Haverfordwest; the priory ruins.

Haverfordwest; reconstruction of the priory church.

100

church early in the 13th century. The space allocated for the priory buildings was a cramped shelf between the steep hillside and the river. In any case the initial layout was very modest, and consisted of a simple cruciform church and three ranges grouped around a cloister. More buildings were added later, including a kitchen and farmery. Current excavations have uncovered a wealth of dressed stonework, and some fragments can be seen *in situ*. Much alas, of the former splendour of the Priory church was lost at the Dissolution, and the decay was helped along by the stone-robbing activities of the townsfolk.

HIGGON'S WELL (116)

This is the most important of several holy wells in the Haverfordwest area. It was once visited by countless pilgrims on the road to St David's, but now has the more prosaic function of supplying spring water to an adjacent soft drinks factory. The mineral water can be bought by the bottle or sampled free from a fountain beside the well. The vaulted well building can be seen at the rear of a modern house, next to a riverside footpath, 1 mile south-east of the town.

HAROLDSTON (117)

Haroldston House is a sad sight today: chunks of tumbled walls, a darkly gaping cellar, thickets of hawthorn and brambles, and over all rears the shell of a three-storey tower house. The building lies within the sight of the rapidly expanding suburbs of Haverfordwest, just east of Merlin's Bridge. A minor road curves around past the ruins providing a good vantage point for those not inclined to get tangled up in the undergrowth.

In its heyday, Haroldston was an extensive and sumptuous mansion, with courtyards, orchards and walled gardens. The oldest part of the house is believed to be the 'Steward's tower', a compact gatehouse with a vaulted ground floor passage, and two upper chambers. Flanking turrets contained garderobes and a newel stair. A short distance away to the west is a vaulted undercroft, which presumably marks the site of the Great Hall. Haroldston was the principal residence of the Perrot family, and birthplace of John Perrot (1527-92), 'Good Sir John', an irascible, boisterous, foulmouthed Elizabethan who ruled this part of Pembrokeshire like a king. And, indeed, he was

almost that, for Perrot has the reputation of being the illegitimate son of Henry VIII. His mother was Mary Berkely, Royal lady-in-waiting, and less-than faithful wife of Thomas Perrot. Poor Thomas had better luck at breeding pheasants than raising a family, for George Owen informs us that these game birds were unknown in Pembrokeshire until Sir Thomas introduced them into 'a pleasant grove of his owne planting adjoining to his house of Haroldston'.

Haroldston continued to be occupied by later members of the Perrot family, but in the early 18th century it was abandoned and leased out to tenants, the beginning of the downward road to neglect and decay.

JOHNSTON CHURCH (118)

This remarkable little church lies only a few yards from the busy A4076, and appears to have been built by an architect who had his measurements mixed-up. The building comprises a chancel, nave, 2 vaulted transepts and a tower — in essence a typical late Medieval Pembrokeshire church, but here everything is greatly scaled-down in size, and the proportions are marred only by the abnormally short transepts. The existing building is probably a 15th-century reconstruction of an earlier church which belonged to Pill Priory (121). Inside, the corbels of the rood-loft remain, and there is a 14th-century cross-slab set into the chancel step. Two-light squints in the chancel arch enable anyone in the transepts to catch a glimpse of the altar. The outlines of a blocked doorway can be seen in the north wall of the nave.

ROSEMARKET (119)

The little village of Rosemarket retains a number of features reflecting its long history. Over 2000 years ago an Iron Age tribe built a strongly-defended settlement on a promontory between two stream valleys. The single bank and ditch which enclosed the fort is now marked by a line of trees at the rear of the parish church. The church marks the next stage in the village's development, for it bears a pre-Norman dedication to the 6th-century St Ishmael. The existing building, however, belongs to the period following the Norman conquest, when the adjacent fort is believed to have been reused as a castle.

In the 12th century the village, mill and surrounding lands were granted to the Knights Hospitallers of Slebech (53). This military organization may have established a residence here, for which a nearby dovecot was built, to provide a steady supply of fresh meat during the winter months. The birds have long flown, but the dovecot still remains, and lies in a field east of the village. The dovecot is typical of many in west Wales (see also 96, 106), and has over 200 nesting holes on the inner wall. Another glimpse of old Rosemarket is afforded by Cross Farm, opposite the church. Although much restored, the building incorporates a vaulted undercroft and first-floor hall, and may have been the dwelling of a wealthy merchant.

LLANGWM (120)

Llangwm is a straggling village on a hillside above an inlet of the Cleddau, 4 miles south-east of Haverfordwest. It is up to the visitor to decide whether the place-name means *Lang Heimr*, 'long village' (Viking) or 'the church of the valley' (Welsh); both names are apt. The Medieval church of St Jerome snuggles into the hillside below the village, a pleasant, well-kept cruciform building of 13th-14th century date. The interior is restrained and tastefully restored, and there are some interesting Medieval graveslabs beside the south transept. The real treasure of Llangwm, however, is the late 14th-century north transept, the Del la Rupe chapel. Passing through the two-bay arcade, the first thing thaat strikes the eye is the finely decorated tomb recesses in the north wall. Beneath the carved canopies are stone effigies of a mantled lady and a knight 'in shining armour'. Beneath the Knight's head is a large jousting helm with a bird's head crest, while the figure's stylish metal-studded shoes rest on a small lion. This effigy is traditionally that of a member of the De la Rupe family, although the bird-crest identifies it as a Nash, of nearby Great Nash House. The transept also contains a beautifully decorated pillar-piscina, with a canopy encrusted with escutcheons.

At one time the village of Llangwm was famed for its oyster fishing trade, but you can no longer buy oysters here for eight pence a hundred. Richard Fenton commented sourly on this 'miserable village' with its 'straggling houses and mountains of oystershells', before hurrying on his

way inland to Great Nash, then 'unroofed and in ruins'. Part of the house has since been rebuilt, but at the rear is a vaulted building reminiscent of the diminutive tower houses at West Tarr and Carswell (91). Sandwiched between later farm buildings nearby is a large and impressive dovecot with a grass-covered roof giving it a thatched look.

PILL PRIORY (121)

There is little enough left now of Pill priory, but what survives is impressive in its own right. One side of the central tower with an arch opening into the vanished chancel stands in the middle of a modern garden, like an abstract sculpture. Part of the adjacent house incorporates some early masonry, but the rest of the monastic complex lies below ground, awaiting the excavator's trowel. The ruins can be seen from the roadside ½ mile north-west of Milford Haven, in a secluded valley beside the railway line. Pill was founded around 1200 by Adam de Rupe of Roch Castle (133) as a cell of St Dogmael's for monks of the Tironian Order. De Rupe also granted to the Priory all the churches on his lands, including Johnston and Steynton. By the early 16th century only a Prior and five monks occupied the House, which was valued at £67 at the Dissolution. The property later passed to the affluent Barlows of Slebech.

WALWYN'S CASTLE (122)

Walwyn's Castle is a cluster of modern houses beside the modern church of St James, just off the B4327 road to Dale. The lower half of the tower is Medieval though, distinguishable by the more rugged stonework. The rest of the building is a tasteful and restrained Victorian idea of what a Medieval church should look like.

From the graveyard a footpath leads south to the hilltop earthworks of the 'castle' of the place-name, a large and impressive Iron Age hillfort with a later motte and bailey inside. The extensive Prehistoric enclosure was divided by the bailey rampart, and the tip of an inner rampart heightened and enlarged to form the base mound of a timber keep. This castle has been linked with an improbable Medieval legend, claiming that the bones of the Arthurian hero, Gwalchmai (Gawain) were dug up here in the time of William the Conqueror. The Tudor antiquarian John Leland reported seeing 'giant bones' unearthed here, and even in

Pill Priory from a 19th century etching.

this century it was confidently stated that the castle was, in fact, a burial mound.

A more substantial hillfort lies 1½ miles to the east besides the Johnston road. This is **Ramus Castle (123)**, better known (misleadingly) as Roman's Castle, a pentagonal enclosure with two lines of defence. The entrance lies between two inturned banks in the south-west side, and the powerful inner rampart stands up to 12 feet high.

ST ISHMAEL'S CHURCH (124)

St Ishmael's was one of the seven Bishop's houses of Dyfed, and the existence of several Dark Age stones in the Medieval church indicates that there was a burial ground here long before the Norman conquest. Two country roads approach the modern village from the north, one passes the tallest standing stone in west Wales at Mabesgate, and the other skirts the mound of a Norman motte castle. The church lies a short distance away from the village in a narrow wooded valley leading down to the sea at Monk Haven. The sloping churchyard is an overgrown wilderness of pine, yew and rhododendron, bisected by a little stream. The existing

building has been extensively restored and is the end product of more than one period of Medieval modification. The nave is flanked by transepts of different sizes, and linked by passage-squints to the chancel. Beside the 12th-century 'cushion' font are three carved stones; two bear simple crosses while the third is part of an elaborate 10th or 11th-century cross — a lone fragment of what must have been a magnificent piece of Dark Age sculpture.

ST BRIDES (125)

St Brides is a remarkable place; a horseshoe of low cliffs sheltering the little bay, scattered cottages brightly painted, the austere hulk of the Medieval church and, in the background, the mock-gothic baronial residence of St Brides 'castle', sheltered in a grove of trees indifferent to the winter storms. The turbulent sea has already claimed the chapel of St Bride, which stood on the low headland north of the church. This small building may well have marked the site of the original Dark Age foundation, for coastal erosion has also uncovered slab-lined graves of Early Christian type.

St Bride (or Brigit) was originally an Irish pagan

fertility gooddess who had the good fortune to be 'converted' and upgraded to saint status by the Early Christians. Although Brigit never left her native haunts, the dedication was bestowed by the Dark Age Irish immigrants. The church stands at the head of the haven, surrounded by an immaculately kept graveyard, and with a fine view of the distant 'Castle'. Before entering the church, visitors should notice a blocked arch on the right of the porch — all that remains of the former south transept. The interior is spacious, but overrestored and harshly whitewashed. The rood loft has long vanished, but its steps and doorway survive in the chancel. In the north transept is a group of Medieval sepulchral monuments; three are set into the floor and bear weathered relief-carvings of recumbent figures. The fourth is a more familiar tomb-effigy of the type already encountered elsewhere in west Wales.

Before leaving this remote point of the coastline it is worth walking a short distance down the wooded drive to the castle where, on either side of the road, can be seen ruined walls and buildings. This is called 'St Brides Abbey', but there is nothing ecclesiastical about the remains, which could well date from the late Middle Ages. A large and spacious oven is a particularly obvious feature, while on the opposite side of the road is the ivy-covered shell of a three-storey building, possibly a modified tower house.

NAB HEAD (126)

Only the earthworks of Tower Point promontory fort on the cliffs west of St Brides survive above ground today, but the adjacent Nab Head was also the site of a Prehistoric settlement. Thousands of flint implements have been discovered on the Head over the years, making this one of the most important Mesolithic sites in Wales. When the headland was occupied by the nomadic hunters and tool makers some 8000 years ago, the sea was at a much lower level, and a broad plain stretched between the campsite and the sea. Thousands of years later in the Iron Age, another settlement was established on nearby Tower Point, then, as now, a sheer-sided promontory above the turbulent sea. Excavations in 1970 revealed that the inner fort rampart was built in two separate phases, and when complete may have stood at least 10 feet high. In the north-east corner of the enclosure a rock-cut

drainage gulley marked the site of a round hut, with a central hearth, and probably turf walls supporting a peaked thatch roof. Both the fort and Mesolithic campsite can be reached from St Brides along the coast path.

GATEHOLM (127)

Gateholm island is a sinuous chunk of rock stretching for almost half a mile into the cold waters of Broad Sound, and which can only be reached at low tide. From the beach a steep and tricky path climbs to the summit of this sheer-sided plateau; the rest of Gateholm is inaccessible from below. Scattered along the length of the island are no fewer than 110 rectangular huts, their foundations outlined by tufts of springy fescue grass. Most of the huts are linked together forming long rows, others have adjoining enclosures and field walls. The population of the island has been optimistically estimated at 150-250, but despite the great number of huts, the largest only measures 10×20 feet inside. One of the huts was excavated in 1930, and it was found to consist of crude turf walls faced with drystone, and a central hearth. Two pits either side of the hearth marked the position of timber posts which supported a thatch or turf roof (see reconstruction drawing).

The great range of finds picked up on the island over the years includes: Prehistoric flint implements, 3rd-century Roman coins, a Dark Age bronze pin, and Medieval potsherds: none of which can conclusively date the numerous huts. The rectangular shape of the dwellings would accord well with a Romano-British date, but a more intriguing possibility is that Gateholm was a Dark Age monastic settlement, similar to the better known establishment at Tintagel in Cornwall. Although none of the surviving huts appears to have been used as a chapel, the monastery theory is very tempting. Standing at the seaward tip of Gateholm, one can just grasp the unerring commitment needed by someone to live on this barren, windswept rock. Who else but a hermit-monk, devoted to the service of God, would possess such selfless devotion and faith?

Further evidence of ancient clifftop habitation is provided by Marloes Sound Rath, a short distance west along the coast path. The fort is enclosed by a series of three ramparts and ditches, now eroded and overgrown, but still of impressive strength.

Gateholm; reconstruction of part of the hut complex.

DEER PARK POINT (128)

The furthermost tip of the Milford peninsula is the site of the largest Iron Age defended settlement in west Wales. The man-made defences consist only of a single crampart crossing the narrow neck of the promontory from Martin's Haven to Renny Slip Bay; but the isolated headland is a huge 300 acres. The 19th-century owners of St Brides Castle attempted to turn the headland into a deer park, and so a long wall was built to keep the deer in, while the Prehistoric wall was meant to keep undesirables out. In 1984 a 7th-9th-century ring-cross was discovered embedded in the wall. The stone is a good indication that there was an Early Christian establishment hereabout (the presumed 'monastery' of Gateholm is not far away), and the cross is now displayed at the adjacent National Trust centre. Visitors approaching the headland should also stop briefly at the little church of Marloes on the way. The existing cruciform building (partially rebuilt around 1874) is said to have replaced an earlier coastal church destroyed by the sea. The barrel-vaulted chancel has the remains of an unusual stone screen separating it from the nave.

St. David's and the Pencaer Peninsula

(Sites 129–150)

RUDBAXTON RATH (129)

This large and impressive 'rath' is a prominent site viewed from the nearby railway. The main line cuts across the slope of the hill on which the fort lies, a clump of trees and bushes mark the position of the defences. A single powerful rampart with a silted-up outer ditch forms an oval enclosure, 320 feet across. The entrance was a simple gap through the bank in the north-east side. Just outside the entrance is a restored holy well and the site of a Medieval chapel dedicated to St. Leonard. Was this chapel established in an attempt to sanctify a 'pagan' area? There are also legends of ghostly hounds and the 'wild hunt' associated with the rath. A more mundane explanation is that the chapel served the spiritual needs of a short-lived Norman settlement, for the rath was adapted as a ringwork and bailey in the 12th century. In a Medieval document the hillfort is named as 'Simon Castle beside the chapel of St Leonards'. The fate of the castle is unrecorded, but the little chapel was still being used to celebrate Mass at the end of the 14th century.

RUDBAXTON (130)

Who can fail to be impressed by Rudbaxton church, with its cheerfully portentious Baroque monument to the Howard family? There they stand, five members of the same family cut off in the prime of life by the plague, the most famous occupants of this Medieval building. The near life-size effigies are carefully painted in subdued colours, and represent George Howard (d. aged 32 in 1665) who points to a skull in his left hand; James (d. aged 35 in 1668), his wife Joanna, and their two children, Thomas (d. 1682) and Mary (d. 1685), both clasping grinning skulls as if about to embark on a macabre game of football. The monument was erected by Joanna in memory of 'her Deare friends & children', and she, alone of the figures, does not hold a skull as a symbol of mortality.

The long-departed Howards should not attract all the visitor's attention. Also within the 14th-century south aisle is a mural tablet to General Sir

Thomas Picton, born in this parish in 1758, and killed at Waterloo. Two corbels on either side of the 13th-century chancel arch have been carved with human faces, the one on the north with a crown. The outside of the church has its interesting features too: several blocked late Medieval windows, and a sundial dated 1689. This venerable building lies about 3 miles north of Haverfordwest, off the A40 road to Fishguard. Visitors approaching the church should notice the hopelessly overgrown remains of the castle mound of the Norman lord of Rudbaxton.

CAMROSE (131)

This secluded Medieval settlement lies 'off the beaten track' in a wooded valley 3 miles north-west of Haverfordwest. The castle and church stand on opposite sides of the valley, with a post-Reformation corn mill in the marshy hollow below. The road to Keeston has unfortunately severed the bailey from the 25 foot-high motte, half hidden in a dense clump of rhododendrons and yews. The motte has been adapted as an ornamental garden feature, and the remains of a spiral path leads up to the stone-walled summit. The 14th-century parish church has not escaped some modernization, but is nevertheless an attractive building, with an unusual octagonal stair turret on the tower. A cushion font of 12th-century date in the nave is a relic of the earlier Norman church. All the windows are modern, but some original blocked openings can be seen in the outside walls. A blocked arch also marks the site of a demolished south transept.

NOLTON (132)

'The church is a low undignified structure and has nothing within or without to demand the attention of the antiquary', wrote Fenton at the beginning of the 19th century. His comments were rather harsh on this occasion, for the small church at Nolton, 6 miles north-west of Haverfordwest, does contain an impressive, through damaged, stone effigy of an armoured knight. Incredible as it may seem, this monument was once used as a gatepost, and at the time of Fenton's visit was lying neglected and uncared for in the churchyard. The nearby rectory incorporates the remains of a Medieval first-floor hall: 'it has marks of great antiquity . . , and was formerly approached by a gateway opening into a

Rudbaxton; the Howard memorial in the south aisle.

quadrangle with walls 5 ft thick', wrote Fenton.

Nearby Nolton Haven was formerly a port for exporting anthracite coal mined locally since the Middle Ages. Some of the cliffside levels are believed to be remnants of Tudor workings.

ROCH CASTLE (133)

Legend-haunted Roch Castle is such a conspicuous landmark that few visitors approaching the St David's peninsula can fail to notice its battlemented silhouette on the skyline. The castle ws reputedly built by Adam de Rupe around 1200, but the existing masonry is a century or so later in date. Adam took the precaution of building his castle on a lofty chunk of volcanic rock to foil a prophecy

that, at a certain date, he would die from the poisonous bite of an adder. In his eyrie-like stronghold, De Rupe may well have felt safe from any reptile; but when the fatal hour arrived his scaly nemesis was inadvertently brought into the castle hidden inside a bundle of firewood.

All that remains of the earlier fortress is a small earthwork bailey at the foot of the rock. The existing tower, of c. 1300 date with 15th-century additions, is D-shaped in plan with a flanking turret on the south side. There are three floors, with small vaulted chambers in the turret. Fenton recorded a tradition that the castle had become ruinous by the time of the last male heir, Thomas de Rupe, in the mid 15th century, but it was restored and passed

Roch Castle.

WOLF'S CASTLE AND THE TREFFGARNE FORTS (134)

The dramatically named 'castle of the wolf' is an undramatic tree-covered mound of a Norman motte and bailey stronghold, which guarded a river crossing at the north end of the rocky Treffgarne gorge. The earthworks can be seen from the A40 just north of the Cleddau bridge.

The narrow gorge in the volcanic rock through which the river, road and railway force a passage has long been a strategic obstacle requiring some additional defence. The motte is only one of a number of fortifications on the surrounding hill-tops. On both sides of the pass are no fewer than eight hillforts, not including the dubious Maiden Castle (an impressive natural outcrop) and another site destroyed by quarrying The most accessible of these fort can be reached by a footpath from Treffgarne to Wolf's Castle, along the west side of the gorge. The poorly-preserved remains at **Poll Cairn** (which some authorities believe may be entirely natural) is said to incorporate a line of *chevaux-dè-frise* on the east, but this dedicated rambler failed to find it. Further north is a small group of round-huts, evidently part of an undefended open settlement. Directly east, on the precipitous edge of the gorge, is a fine example of an inland promontory fort. The defences are massed only on the west and south sides, the remainder of the enclosure being more than adequately defended by the steep rocky slopes.

THE PENCAER PENINSULA (135-138)

Aside from Prehistoric monuments (of which there is a surfeit), the Pencaer Peninsula has much to offer the visitor to west Wales. From the bleak and rugged hills to the spectacular coastal scenery at Pwllderi and Strumble Head, there is a wealth of natural beauty here. The windswept promontory of Carregwastad was the site of the last invasion of Britain, in 1797, while on the nearby crags are several Iron Age hillforts built for defence against invaders in far earlier times. The rich crop of archaeological sited here has long attracted the attention of antiquarians, including Richard Fenton ('Druidical monuments and other ancient works meet you here at every turn', he wrote) and Edward Llwyd. Over a dozen megalithic and Prehistoric monuments are to be found in the hills

into a long succession of owners. Roche was the home of the 17th-century Walters family, whose daughter, Lucy, was a mistress of Charles II and mother of his illegitimate son, the Duke of Monmouth. During the Civil War the castle was held by Royalists. There is a story (not very reliable) that during the siege the Royalist commander spied Cromwell on horse-back, and threw a javelin at him. The javelin passed so close that it cut the strap of Cromwell's helmet, causing him to gallop away in some alarm.

By the early 19th century the castle had been reduced to a picturesque ruin, but around 1900 it was purchased and restored by John Philipps, First Viscount St David's. Roch now offers self-catering accommodation for those who fancy an adder-free holiday with a difference.

between Goodwick and Pwllder, and those described below are the most accessible.

At **Carn Wen**, (135) behind a row of houses above Goodwick harbour, are three ruined Neolithic burial chambers; the southernmost is the best preserved and is known as Carreg Samson. From Carn Wen a road leads west to Llanwnda, passing another burial chamber on the right at Penrhiw Farm. High among the rocks overlooking Llanwnda village is yet another Neolithic tomb, also called Carreg Samson. Like other sub-megalthic tombs, this burial chamber was formed by raising and underpining a natural boulder. The large capstone is propped up over a rock-cut pit, in which a small urn filled with burnt bones was discovered many years ago. A short distance to the south is the Park Henner standing stone, an 8 foot-high slab set up in the Bronze Age.

The **Medieval church of St Wnda** (136) was practically rebuilt in 1881, but it retains several relics of the earlier building. One of the 15th-century roof trusses has a carved head of a tonsured priest. Another face, carved at least 1000 years ago, peers from a stone slab set into the outside wall of the south chapel. The face may represent the Virgin Mary, but it is not a comforting, inspiring image, for the features strongly echo the sculptural styles of the pagan Celts. Four other cross-stones of c. 600-800 AD can be found by looking carefully at the stones embedded in the outside walls. All are relics of a pre-Norman burial ground.

Leaping back a further 2000 years in time, but travelling a mere 1½ miles in distance, we arrive at another group of megalithic monuments at **Carn Gilfach** (137). On the south side of the hill a 14 foot-long slab marks the site of a Neolithic burial chamber. Peer underneath the stone and you will see that it forms the underpinned capstone of a very low burial chamber. On the upper surface of this 'altar'-like stone are several small hollows, which Fenton naïvely assures us were 'probably intended to have received the blood of the victim', but which today fill with more sinister than rainwater. At Lady's Gate on the north side of Carn Gilfach is a fallen monolith, almost 11 feet-long. There was a second standing stone here at one time, and there is also a legend of buried treasure guarded by a phantom lady. Perhaps to substaniate the tale, Fenton excavated around the stones but found nothing (which is hardly surprising considering the crude archaeological techniques of the early 19th century).

Further west, the landscape changes dramatically as the igneous outcrops rear to greater heights before plunging into the sea at Pwllderi. Monuments of the Iron Age now dominate the landscape. The small defended settlements of Dinas Mawr, Castell Poeth, Gaer Fach and Ysgubor Gaer are all overshadowed in size and importance by **Gaer Fawr** (138), one of the most impressive of the stone-walled forts of west Wales. The fort was first described and surveyed by Edward Llwyd around 1700, with remarkable detail and accuracy for the time. The initial defences comprised a drystone wall with an inturned entrance on the east. Additional walls were later built on the east and west sides. The fort may have been occupied into the Roman period, although several oblong huts could be the remains of Medieval peasant's dwellings.

RHOS Y CLEGYRN AND FFYST SAMSON (139)

Looking like a misplaced trillithon from Stonehenge, Ffyst Samson is surely the most bizzare Neolithic tomb in Wales. The burial chamber has been so robbed of material that only two upright slabs remain, supporting a lopsided capstone 6 feet above ground. The tomb lies near the summit of a hill ½ mile south-east of St Nicholas village, and can be reached by paths from the road, or the nearby moor of Rhos y Clegyrn.

Of the complex ritual structures revealed by excavation at **Rhos y Clegyrn**, only a tall monolith and a gorse-covered cairn are visible today. The 9 foot-high stone was found to have been one of a pair that stood at the edge of an oval area of cobbled stones; beneath thws was a group of at least seven crudely built huts of possible Neolithic date. Long before the construction of the Bronze Age ritual monuments this moor was the site of a temporary settlement, perhaps used only during the summer months. Fenton saw 'a large Druidical circle' here, which suggests that the nearby cairn may have been an embanked stone circle (see 78). Another impressive Bronze Age monolith can be seen from the roadside at Ffynnondrudion, 1 mile to the north-east. The Medieval parish church of St Nicholas is also worth visiting while in the district. The restored building contains three Dark

Age inscribed stones, one unusually commemorating a lady: 'Tunnccetace, wife of Daarus'.

MATHRY (140)

Mathry church is situated on a breezy hilltop overlooking the main Fishguard to St David's road. The village is grouped neatly about the parish church, which was rebuilt in 1869. The stunted tower was originally topped with a steeple (a useful landmark for mariners) until a storm knocked it down. According to legend the church was founded by seven saints, who were born to a local woman all at once. After that alarming experience the poor woman tried to drown them like kittens, but St Teilo rescued the children and brought them up in the faith. A relic of the Dark Age foundation is an inscribed stone which was set up around 500 AD, in memory of Maccudiccl, son of Caticuus. The top line of the inscription has gone, but it was fortunately recorded by Edward Llwyd. Faint traces of an Ogham inscription can be seen along the edge of the slab. Two more cross-stones of the Dark Ages have been set into the churchyard wall opposite the nave.

One more Early Christian monument needs to be singled out, the well-known **Mesur y Dorth** stone, which is built into a roadside wall 2½ miles further west near Croesgoch. The name means 'the measure of the loaf', after a belief that pilgrims to St David's would place their bread rations against the ring-cross to see if they had enough to last out the journey. A variation of this story tells how St David set up the stone to serve as an indicator of bread size during a food shortage. In fact, the stone has nothing to do with bread, for it was set up between 600 and 800 AD to mark the grave of a local dignitary.

CARREG SAMSON BURIAL CHAMBER (141)

This impressive Neolithic tomb has an equally impressive location: a sloping headland overlooking Abercastle Bay and the Pencaer peninsula. It can be reached from the coast path, or a road to Longhouse Farm, ¾ mile north-east of Trefin. It was constructed about 5000 years ago as a mausoleum for the local farming tribes. Only the gaunt chamber now remains, but this would originally have been surrounded by a cairn of stones, and approached along a slab-lined covered passage.

The cairn may have been encircled with a kerb of upright slabs, for antiquarians reported seeing two 'stone circles' surrounding the tomb. Excavations in 1968 revealed that the burial chamber itself had been raised over a rock-cut pit which had been deliberately filled in (a curious ritual feature also observed at Pentre Ifan (62)).

On the sea cliffs beyond the tomb is an Iron Age promontory fort known as Castell Coch, one of three similarly named forts on this stretch of the coastline. A more impressive promontory fort is **Caerau** (142) near Abereiddy, a two-period site, with an inner bank and ditch enclosure to which was later added a western annexe and an additional line of outer defences.

BRAWDY CHURCH (143)

Since the construction of the nearby RAF base, the Medieval parish church of Brawdy is hardly one of the most tranquil places in west Wales. But a hallowed air imbues this ancient place despite the unwelcome attentions of low-flying jets and helicopters. The church is reached along a lane from Rhyd-y-gele, and consists of a long, low building, with a chancel, nave and a lengthy south chapel. The masonry is mostly 13th century with later work, although the building was restored in the 19th century. Within are kept three memorial slabs of c. 500 AD, all brought here from elsewhere in the parish. None of the Latin inscriptions is complete, and only the names survive: 'Quagte', 'Briacus' and 'Vendognus'. We have Edward Llwyd to thank for recording the latter name, for the inscription is now illegible.

SOLFA (144)

Solfa was formerly a haven for smugglers and pirates, and it may well have been for security against such freebooters that an Iron Age tribe fortified their headland camp, around 2000 years ago. Whatever the reasons, the earthworks of their defended settlement still survive on the Gribyn, a narrow ridge which separates the two 'drowned valleys' at Solfa. The earthworks of a larger enclosure lie further north along the ridge. The modern village of Solfa has moved away from the original settlement, which was probably in the vicinity of the old parish church at St Elvis, ½ mile further east. The church has long been destroyed, and an adjacent Neolithic burial chamber is a shapeless jumble of stones. The modern parish church contains a large ring-cross of c. 600-800 AD, which was brought from the ruined Medieval building.

CASTELL PENPLEIDIAU (145)

A classic example of a promontory fort, situated on the east side of Caerfai Bay near St David's. The seaward tip of this long headland has been isolated by three strong ramparts and ditches, drawn across the ridge from cliff to cliff. Anyone entering the camp would have had to pass along the narrow 'corridor' between the east end of the banks and the sheer cliff edge. These defences now enclose only a fragment of land, since erosion has left a deep gash across the interior.

Coastal erosion has also demolished the occupational area of the larger and more impressive **Porth-y-rhaw** (146) fort, 1½ miles further east. Visitors can obtain a near-'bird's eye' view of the site from the higher promontory on the west. Fenton carried out a small excavation in the interior, and discovered a hearth site and a heap of limpet shells, the remains of a modest Iron Age meal. The antiquarian also saw numerous hut sites betwen the outer ramparts, although nothing can be traced of these today. In the great cauldron of cliffs beneath the fort are several battered hulks of wrecked ships, victims (like the fort itself) of the restless and destructive power of the sea.

ST DAVID'S CATHEDRAL (147)

'And so we came to the end of the world where the patron Saint of Wales sleeps by the western sea', wrote Francis Kilvert in his diary, October 1871. And what a remarkable place St David's is: a village pretending to be a city, houses and cottages clustered about the green and 14th-century cross, the rambling ruins of the Bishop's Palace, and the great cathedral itself, dominating all and nothing. Its presence is indicated to the approaching visitor by the 16th-century pinnacles of the tower, glimpsed at the far end of the village (or rather, city) street. From the high cross the road wanders down the hillside to the cathedral, providing magnificent views not only of the venerable building itself, but also the bleak Dewisland peninsula, the flat landscape punctuated by an occasional upthrust of volcanic rock.

Most visitors enter the precinct through Porth-y-twr, the only remaining Medieval gateway which incorporates an octagonal bell-tower on the north side. 39 steps descend the green hillside to the great church, which was reputedly built in such a low-lying spot to avoid its tower being spotted by the sea-roving vikings. But the original church founded by Saint David (Dewi Sant) in the 6th century would hardly have attracted the attention of pagan pillagers even had it been built on high ground. Nothing now survives of that little building, for the existing noble structure dates from the 12th to 16th centuries, with a liberal amount of 19th-century restoration work.

David's attempts at unobtrusively building a church in a hidden valley did not meet with initial success. The pagan chieftan of Clegyr Boia hillfort proved a stubborn obstacle to the saint's religious schemes, and later, in the 10th and 11th centuries, the church suffered the wrath of pagan invaders no less than ten times. In 999 Bishop Morgenau was killed in a Viking raid (a divine punishment, we are told, for the Bishop's un-monastic habit of eating meat), and as late as 1080, the year before William the Conqueror visited St David's Bishop Abraham was likewise a victim of the Norsemen. The period of native control at St David's came to an end in 1115, when the first in a line of Norman Bishops was elected.

The building which today confronts the visitors embodies work of more than one period, and is the culmination of almost 3½ centuries of rebuilding and extensions. The long nave is a majestic structure, with ponderous Norman arches and pillars (leaning out and sloping up — an indication that building a cathedral in a marshy valley is not a sound idea), finely carved *pulpitum* screen, and over all a flat oak roof enlivened with carved arches and pendants. Again, this is work of more than one period: the nave walls are late 12th century, the screen 14th century, and the roof late 15th-early 16th century. Throughout the building the observant visitor can detect several architectural styles and masonry work of different phases.

All that survives of the pre-Norman settlement is a collection of inscribed and carved stones, mostly Celtic crosses of 10th and 11th-century date. The rebuilding of the early cathedral began in ernest under Bishop Peter de Leia in 1180. Peter chose a curiously archaic transitional Norman style with heavy round arches decorated with chevrons

St. David's Cathedral.

the canons to undertake the enlarging of the Norman church. The chapel of St Thomas was added to the north transept, chapels were built eastwards of the high altar, followed by the Lady Chapel around 1300. Later in the 14th century St Thomas' Chapel was heightened into a tower-like three stories, and an extra stage was added to the central tower. In 1365 Bishop Houghton founded a college of priests to ensure that divine offices were properly sung. The collegiate buildings lay to the north of the nave, but today only the restored St Mary's chapel and the cloister walls survive. The latter part of the 15th century witnessed a renewed effort to increase the splendour of the cathedral, but in wood rather than stone. The aforementioned nave roof was constructed by William Pole, Treasurer of St David's (1470-1509) who may also have been responsible for the magnificent choir stalls and the canopied Bishop's throne. Underneath the stall seats are misericords, or 'mercy rests', projecting ledges which enabled the canons to rest in an upright position during the long services. With these misericords the Medieval carver let his imagination run riot, for they are carved with a variety of secular subjects — a wolf in a monk's cowl, two men building a ship, another pair suffering from backache, a sinister pre-Christian 'green man', and a group of sea-sick pilgrims. One of the stalls is reserved for the sovereign of Britain (who has always been a member of the cathedral chapter), although the present monarch has never occupied it.

Within the walls of this great building lie the mortal remains of saints, hermits and princes. Gerald of Wales is reputed to be buried here, a fitting tribute if it is true, for all his life Gerald strove vigorously to become bishop of St David's, one step in the direction of his dream of establishing a Welsh Church independent of Canterbury. There are dozens of tombs, effigies and memorial slabs throughout the cathedral, and only a few can be mentioned here. Beside the 14th-century *Pulpitum* is the worn and mutilated effigy of Bishop Henry de Gower (1328-47), an enthusiastic builder whose main memorial is the Palace across the river. A tomb-effigy of similar date can be found in the south choir aisle: an armed knight reputed to be the effigy of the 12th-century Welsh prince, Rhys ap Gruffudd. The coat of arms of the princely house, a lion rampant, is emblazoned on the figure's sur-

and dog-tooth moulding, at a time when the lighter, graceful Gothic style was already in use in England. The plan was a typical cruciform building with high-pitched roofs: a nave, chancel, transepts, with a squat central tower over the crossing. Work would still have been in progress when a preaching campaign, headed by Archbishop Baldwin and Gerald of Wales arrived in 1188. 'in St Davids we were given good accommodation by Peter, the Bishop of that Diocese, a most friendly and hospitable man'. Those words must have cost Gerald dearly, for Peter was Gerald's rival in his bid for the bishopric.

The marshy nature of the ground bedevilled the cathedral architects even into the 19th century. In 1120 most of the tower collapsed and had to be rebuilt, while in the 15th century the drastically leaning nave walls were propped up by a series of buttresses. The sole remaining Norman arch of the tower also had to be reconstructed to prevent its collapse, during the 19th-century restorations.

In the 13th century the increasing revenues from pilgrim's offerings at the shrine of St David enabled

St. David's; the magnificent Cathedral, with the Bishop's Palace in the background.

St. David's Cathedral; sea-sick pilgrims on a misericord.

coat. In front of the high altar in the presbytery stands the 15th-century altar-tomb of Edmund Tudor, Earl of Richmond. This is not an original cathedral monument; it was brought from the Carmarthen Grey Friars church at the Dissolution, by the order of Edmund's grandson, Henry VIII.

The last of the great building Bishops was Edward Vaughan (1509-23), who roofed over the open court between the presbytery and Lady Chapel, to form the Chapel of the Holy Trinity. A recess in the west wall of this chapel (once the outside wall of the cathedral) contains an oak casket with the bones of Saints David, Caradog and Justinian. These relics were walled up in the recess at the time of the Dissolution and were only discovered during repair work in 1866. Bishop Vaughan also added the third stage to the tower, brining it to its present height of 125 feet.

With the Reformation came changes. The colleges and chantry chapels were dissolved and unroofed, and pilgrimages to the cathedral and subordinate chapels discouraged. Parts of the cathedral were left to ruin, and the great palace was also abandoned. The main body of the church was kept in a tolerable state of repair during the post-Medieval period. When Daniel Defoe visited St David's around 1724, he wrote: 'the venerable aspect of this cathedral church, shews that it has been a beautiful building, but that it is much decay'd'. In 1793 John Nash rebuilt the crumbling west front in a widely disliked style, but the great period of restoration took place after 1860 under the direction of Sir George Gilbert Scott, who replaced Nash's west front with a more typical Norman facade. Repair and restoration work has continued almost to the present day, so that now, after five centuries of decay, this great cathedral, 'at the end of the world', is accessible in its entirety to latter-day pilgrims.

The Bishop's Palace

This is justly reckoned to be one of the finest examples of Medieval domestic architecture in Britain. Although roofless, the building is substantially intact, even though it was dismantled at the Reformation over 400 years ago. The palace was a visible symbol of the relative affluence of the Bishops of St David's, and it must have awed the poor pilgrims on their way to the shrine. Some form of dwelling must have existed here from the earliest days of the cathedral, but the oldest masonry is a range of austere 12th-century buildings. However, by the end of the 13th century the humble dwelling proved inadequate to the needs of Bishops Bek and Martyn, and during their episcopate, a substantial portion of the palace was built. In the second quarter of the 14th century Bishop Gower added a huge new hall (the grandfather of all the vaulted first-floor halls in Wales), and unified the earlier work by constructing decorative parapets and arcaded wall-walks on all the roofs. This architectural motif was also used by De Gower at Lamphey (98), but here the work is far finer, and the parapets are inlaid with a checker pattern of different coloured stones.

On the hilltop a short way downriver of the palace is a much less ostentatious relic of the Norman presence at St David's. In a field on the left of the Porth Clais road can be seen the earthworks of a large ringwork and bailey castle, built, no doubt, to guard against any Welsh uprising from troubling this remote, sacred area of the country.

ST NON'S CHAPEL (148)

The great veneration attached to the shrine of St David is indicated by the former recognition that two pilgrimages here were the equivalent of one to Rome. This importance is further attested by numerous subordinate chapels in the vicinity, which received the prayers and coins of devout, but understandably nervous, pilgrims embarking for Ireland and other coastal destinations. The amount received from these chapels was fairly substantial. George Owen, writing some sixty years after the Dissolution, states that money was brought by the dishful to the cathedral to be divided among the canons, 'the quantity not allowing them leisure to tell it'. Today the ruins of only two of these chapels survive above ground. The best known is St Non's, a small, clifftop ruin, reputed to be the birthplace of St David. The building is dedicated to the saint's mother, Non, and is mentioned in a 14th-century document as the 'chapel of the Blessed Non'. In one corner of the chapel is a ring-cross of c. 600-800 AD which may have come from a pre-Norman burial ground here. A short distance uphill is a small, vaulted holy well. As late as the 19th century the spring water was widely sought after to cure a variety of illnesses, including rheumatism, headaches and eye complaints.

ST JUSTINIAN'S CHAPEL (149)

This is another of the ruined subordinate chapels, but a more substantial survivor. The existing building was constructed by Bishop Vaughan in the early 16th century, and consists of a single chamber with a battlemented parapet, and a bell-tower on the north-west corner. It overlooks the bleak, off-shore mass of Ramsey Island where, according to tradition, St Justinian was murdered by his irate followers. Excavations in 1923 beneath the floor of the chapel revealed the foundations of a small building, which itself had been raised over the stone-lined grave of an earlier cemetery.

The road to St Justinian's point from St David's passes the craggy, volcanic outcrop of Clegyr Boia, the site of an Iron Age hillfort and Neolithic settlement. Further along the road is Rhosson Uchaf farm, one of the few surviving late Medieval peasants' houses of the Dewisland peninsula. There were formerly more, distinguished by their massive conical chimneys, and 'outshuts' — small projecting chambers contained under extensions of the roof. Unlike the upper class first-floor halls, these buildings were 'hall-houses', with a single large ground floor room heated by the great lateral fireplaces. Garn, Llanychaer (71) is another little modified example of this rapidly vanishing house type.

ST DAVID'S HEAD (150)

The historic St David's peninsula is the westernmost point of Wales, and the rugged headland of Penmaen Dewi — St David's Head — might well be regarded as the Welsh Land's End. This jagged finger of rock was known to the 2nd-century Roman geographer, Ptolemy, as *Octopitarum Promontarium*, the promontory of eight perils; a reference to the dangerous reef known as The Bishop and his Clerks. 'The preach deadly doctrine to their winter audience, such poor seafaring men as are forcyd thither by tempest', wrote George Owen around 1600. The headland is now owned by the National Trust and can be reached by a public footpath from the car park at Whitesands Bay. A few yards along the path, a mound on the left marks the site of **St Patrick's chapel**. Excavations in 1924

St. David's Head; a ruined Neolithic tomb at the 'Land's End' of Wales.

uncovered the foundations of this small building, preserved beneath blown sand. The skeletal remains of at least six individuals were found beneath the floor of the chapel, indicating that it had been built on top of an existing burial ground (see also 72, 149). No dating evidence was found, although the excavators suggested that the chapel was built sometime between 500-900 AD.

Beyond the chapel the coast path crosses the rocky flank of **Carn Llidi**, and a poorly-defined footpath leads up to the summit. Behind the ruins of a World War II radar station are two Neolithic burial chambers of the 'sub-megalithic' type, their capstones propped up over rock-cut pits.

On the slopes of nearby Carn Twlc is a large rounded boulder known as *Maen Sigl*, the rocking stone. George Owen considered this to be one of the 'diverse wonders' of the county: 'this stone is mounted upon diverse other stones . . . and is soe equallye poysed as that with one finger a man maye soe shake it, as that you maye sensiblye see it move'. Unfortunately the boulder no longer shakes at a fingers's touch. Looking north the keen-eyed visitor should be able to make out old stone field walls and boundaries criss-crossing the sides of a small stream valley. Although some of the walls are still in use today, they were originally built in the Iron Age or Roman period, probably by the pastorialists who lived in the promonotory fort at the very tip of the headland. The track to the fort passes **Coetan Arthur**, an impressive ruined burial chamber with its capstone supported by a sole remaining upright slab. The remain of a round cairn surrounding the tomb can also be traced.

The people who lived and farmed in this remote area about 2000 years ago defended their headland settlement by constructing a powerful stone-faced rampart across the neck of the ridge. The 8 foot-wide entrance gap was approached by a kerbed causeway across the shallow outer ditch. Within the fort can be seen six or seven stone hut foundations, all that remains of the homes of the resilient families who lived on this most bleak and distant clifftop in the westernmost part of Wales.

Suggested Tours

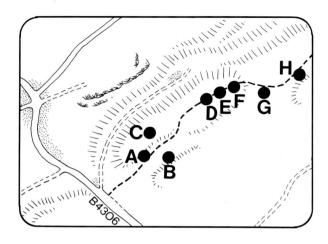

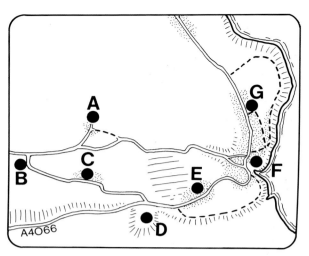

WALK 1: MYNYDD LLANGYNDEIRN

This is the shortest of these 'self-guided' walks, but Mynydd Llangyndeirn is nevertheless an area packed with Prehistoric monuments. The walk begins from the lay-by on the highest part of the B4306, ½-mile uphill of Crwbin village. Follow a rough track to the north-east between two out-cropping ridges to reach the first site of historic interest, an impressive Bronze Age standing stone (A). Against the base of the outcrop to the east is a ruined cairn (B), while on higher ground due north is a second, smaller stone (C). Continue along the path to the summit of the hill where, on a clear day, extensive views of the surrounding countryside are gained. A ring of boulders marks the site of a kerbed cairn (D), with a nearby low mound (E) possibly the remains of another burial mound. There is another cairn on the summit (F), while on low ground to the north-east is a ring cairn (G) with a sunken central area. Just beyond is a rock outcrop with the remains of two ruined Neolithic tombs (H) at its foot. This marks the end of the trail, although two more cairns can be reached further along the ridge.
Length: ¾ mile (each way)

WALK 2: LAUGHARNE & LLANDAWKE

This tour can either be followed on foot or by car, and starts at the coastal town of Laugharne on the Taf estuary. From the square a narrow lane leads west along a wooded valley and then out onto the open countryside. A right turning leads to Llandawke church (A), while the main road goes left to Pendine. Take the next turning on the left, passing Parc y Gerrig Sanctaidd (B), to the rebuilt church of Llansadyrnin (C). The building is Victorian in date, but it contains a Dark Age stone. Continue along from the church to where the road joins the main A4066. The limestone hill on the right is the site of Coygen cave and hillfort (D), now quarried away. The way back to Laugharne is to the left, passing through Broadway village and the site of Roche Castle (E). Between Roche and Llansadyrnin are remains of Medieval 'strip fields', just visible from the road. In Laugharne itself there is the castle (F), the interior presently closed for repair, and the imposing parish church (G) just off the St Clears road.
Length: 4½ miles.

WALK 3: PRESELI MOUNTAINS (EAST)

There are numerous tracks criss-crossing the expanse of the Preseli Mountains and the one highlighted here is only part of a much longer route which can be followed along the spine of the mountains. In any upland area like this, adequate footware, maps and a compass are neccessary. The walk begins at a road junction west of Crymmyrch. A rough track (Prehistoric in origin) leaves the road at Croesmihangel, where there is a much damaged burial mound (A). More apparent is the craggy height of Foeldrygarn (B), crowned by tumbled stone ramparts and three cairns. A number of poorly-defined footpaths lead up to the summit.

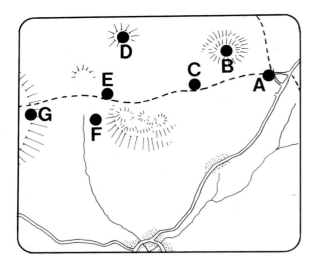

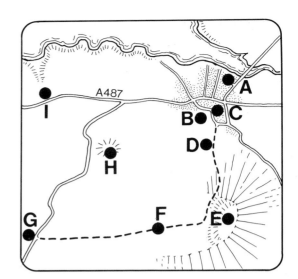

Continue along the main ridgeway route past Carn Ferched (C) to the saw-toothed backdrop of Carn Meini, source of the Stonehenge bluestones. Away to the north is Carn Alw (D) hillfort, while there are two small cairns (E) beside the path, and a ruined burial chamber (F) in the valley below. On the opposite slope of the Corscewgyll valley is Bedd Arthur (G) ritual circle, which marks the end of this particular walk, although the track can be followed for a further 3 miles, passing several more Bronze Age cairns.

Length: 3 miles (each way).

WALK 4: NEWPORT & CARN INGLI COMMON

A more strenuous walk and one that should not be tackled lightly. Adequate footware is advisable. There are several historic sites in Newport itself which can be explored in an hour or so; Carreg Coetan burial chamber (A), the castle (B – exterior only), and the parish church (C). From the church a lane leads uphill, past St Curig's Well (D), and on up to the Common. Carn Ingli hillfort (E) occupies the summit of a rocky outcrop, 1138 feet above sea level, and can be reached by several steep paths. From the summit a level track leads west across the Common, skirting several hut circles and burial mounds, including Carn Briw (F), before joining the mountain road from Pontfaen to Newport. Bedd Morris standing stone (G) is a prominent object here. The road now descends towards Newport, passing a smaller fort at Carn Ffoi (H), to join with the A487 a third of a mile west of the

town. Visitors travelling on to Fishguard can stop (traffic permitting) to look at Cerrig y Gof burial chamber (I) in a field on the right, ¾ mile past the junction.

Length: 5 miles.

WALK 5: ST FLORENCE & THE RITEC VALLEY

This route follows the winding inland course of the Ritec river, and makes a pleasant summer evening's excursion from Tenby. From the railway viaduct below the town take the B4318 towards Carew. Where the road passes the marshy valley bottom, a lay-by and footpath on the right mark the way to Scotsborough (A). The path to the house is muddy at times, and so suitable footware may be needed. Half a mile further along the road is Gumfreston church (B), also reached via a short walk from a lay-by. Continue along to Manor House Wildlife Park, where a turning on the left brings you to maze-like village of St Florence (C). The parish church is an unmistakeable building in the middle of the village, but several Medieval houses with round chimneys need to be hunted down in the adjacent streets. Two roads return to Tenby; the higher ridgeway offers a scenic route to Penally (F), while the lower road passes the tower house at West Tarr (D) (off a minor track in a valley bottom), and Hoyles Mouth Cave (E) before the Treffloyne turning. There is some limited roadside parking space, and a rough path winds up to the cave. A torch is needed for full exploration.

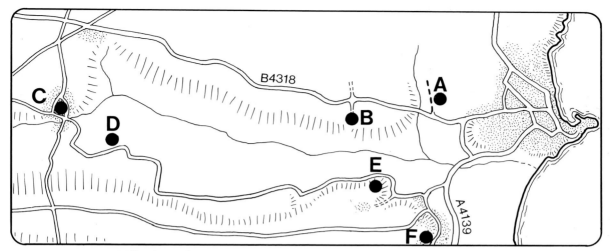

Further on, the road joins the A4139 midway between Tenby and Penally.
Length: 6-7 miles.

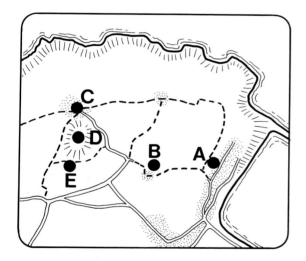

WALK 6: GOODWICK & LLANWNDA

This walk starts off in fairly mundane territory (the Goodwick ferry terminal) but ends up in some typically rocky west Pembrokeshire scenery. From Goodwick follow the road up to Carn Wen overlooking the harbour. Three burial chambers (A) can be seen at the rear of a row of houses. From here a path leads west to Penrhiw Farm, passing another burial chamber (B) in a field on the right. Where the path joins a minor road, turn right for Llanwnda village. The rebuilt church (C) contains a number of Dark Age stones, while in the rocks

above the village is yet another Neolithic tomb (D). Behind the tomb is a natural rock pillar imagined by some antiquarians to have been a 'Druid idol'. A footpath skirts the west edge of the hillside and passes close to the impressive Park Henner standing stone (E). From here return to Goodwick along the main road from Henner Cross, or continue the walk along the backbone of the Pencaer peninsula to Gaer Fawr and Pwllderi in the west.
Length: 3½ miles.

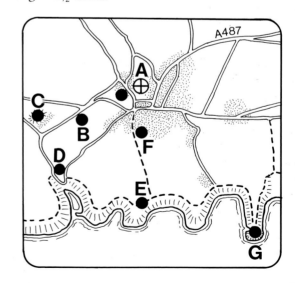

WALK 7: ST DAVID'S & ST NON'S BAY

There are several pleasant walks in the vicinity of the Cathedral city itself; this one takes in a larger area for the more adventurous visitor. Follow the road to St Justinian's past the Cathedral and

Bishop's Palace (A). After a short distance the road forks, and take the left turn for Porthclais. The earthworks of a Medieval castle (B) can be seen on the left, and further on the rocky crag of Clegyr Boia (C) appears on the right. The summit of this small hillfort is accessible from the road next to a much-modernised Medieval farmhouse of the same name. Back on the main route, the road soon dips into Porthclais, passing the overgrown site of a holy well (D) St David was reputedly baptised at. On the east side of the bay the coast path weaves along the clifftop to the ruined chapel and holy well of St Non's (E). A modern chapel contains stones from the long vanished Whitewell (F), a hospice established in the 13th century. Only a few mounds and a spring can be seen of this today, in a field on the right of the road leading back to St David's. For the more dedicated rambler, the coast path continues on to Solfa, passing two Iron Age forts at Castell Penpleidiau (G) and Porth y Rhaw.

Length: 3 miles

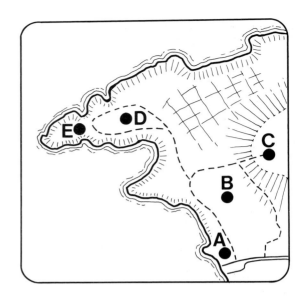

WALK 8: ST DAVID'S HEAD

Penmaen Dewi, St David' Head, is the Welsh Land's End, and the entire promontory is National Trust property. From the car park at Whitesands Bay, a well-marked footpath leads north along the coastline, passing the site of St Patrick's chapel (A), and gradually climbing the rocky flank of Carn Llidi. A short distance off the path is Maen Sigl (B), the rocking stone, a huge boulder which unfortunately no longer moves. A vague path climbs up to the summit of Carn Llidi where two small burial chambers (C) can be found at the base of a rock outcrop. Looking north from here, traces of ancient field walls and boundaries can be seen. Returning to the main coast path the way ahead is across a marshy valley and then up along the side of the headland. Coetan Arthur burial chamber (D) is another relic of Prehistoric activity in this area, while at the tip of the promontory are clustered hut circles and defensive ramparts of an Iron Age farmstead (E).

Length: 1½ miles (each way).

CLASSIFIED LIST OF SITES AND MONUMENTS

Paleolithic cave sites

35 Coygen (SN 284091)
92 Hoyle's Mouth (SN 112002)
94 Caldey caves (SS 145970)
101 Priory Farm cave (SM 979017)

Neolithic burial chambers

6 Llangyndeirn (SN 485133)
9 Myrddin's Quoit (SN 377154)
10 Twlc y filiast (SN 337160)
40 Morfa Bychan (SN 223075)
62 Pentre Ifan (SN 100370)
63 Bedd yr afanc (SN 108346)
65 Coetan Arthur (SN 060394)
66 Cerrig y gof (SN 037389)
78 Carn Besi (SN 156276)
79 Gwal y filiast(SN 170256)
85 Carn Turne (SM 980272)
96 King's quoit (SS 060973)
105 Devil's quoit (SM 886008)
135 Carn Wen (SM 948390)
136 Carn Wnda (SM 933393)
137 Carn Gilfach (SM 910390)
139 Ffyst Samson (SM 906349)
141 Carreg Samson (SM 848335)
150 Carn Llidi (SM 735278)
150 Coetan Arthur (SM 725280)

Bronze Age burial mounds

6 Llangyndeirn (SN 483133)
22 Crug yr ast (SN 359320)
30 Llanboidy (SN 194229)
44 Crug Swllt (SN 177124)
58 Frenni Fawr (SN 200350)
67 Carn Briw (SN 056371)
74-77 Preseli cairns
77 Foel Drygarn (SN 157336)
82 Dyffryn cairn circle (SN 059285)
83 Castlebythe mountain (SN 027297)
100 Dry Burrows (SR 950997)
100 Corston Beacon (SR 933998)
105 Kilpaison Burrows (SM 890007)

Standing stones & circles

6 Llangyndeirn (SN 480130)
18 Nantgaredig henge (SN 495212)
20 Meini Gwyn (SN 459261)
64 Tafarn y Bwlch (SN 083337)
68 Bedd Morris (SN 037364)
69 Lady Stone (SM 996376)
74 Cerrig Meibion Arthur (SN 118310)
75 Gors fawr circle (SN 134294)
76 Bedd Arthur circle (SN 134324)
78 Buarth Arthur circle (SN 142266)
78 Castell Garw (?) henge (SN 147269)
112 Devil's Quoit (SS 981951)
124 Mabesgate (SM 827077)
136 Parc Henner (SM 933390)
137 Carn Gilfach (SM 908392)
139 Rhos y Clegyrn (SM 913354)
139 Ffynnon-drudion (SM 921364)

Iron Age hillforts and defended settlements

11 Castell Cogan (SN 327130)
12 Llangynog (SN 336166)
13 Llansteffan (SN 351101)
17 Merlin's Hill (SN 455216)
29 Hafod camp (SN 218226)
35 Coygen fort (SN 284091)
41 Top Castle (SN 194077)
50 Caerau gaer (SN 139161)
50 Llanddewi gaer (SN 144161)
51 Robeston Wathen (SN 077155)
59 Bayvil Gaer (SN 113417)
60 Castell Henllys (SN 118390)
65 Newport (SN 058396)
67 Carn Ingli (SN 063373)
77 Foel Drygarn (SN 157336)
77 Carn Ffoi (SN 048379)
82 Henry's Moat (SN 044274)
83 Cas-fuwch (SN 024291)
86 Spittal Rath (SM 978229)
87 Castell Buckette (SM 950310)
107 Sheep Island (SM 845017)
108 Castlemartin (SR 914983)
109 Flimston forts (SR 930945)
112 Fishponds camp (SR 971948)
112 Greenala point (SS 007965)
119 Rosemarket Rath (SM 952080)
122 Walwyn's Castle (SM 073030)
123 Roman's Castle (SM 895106)
126 Nab Head (SM 790108)
127 Marloes Sound Rath (SM 768079)
128 Deer Park Point (SM 757090)
129 Rudbaxton Rath (SM 984188)
134 Treffgarne gorge forts (SM 95-24-)
138 Gaer Fawr (SM 894388)
142 Caerau (SM 787308)
144 Solfa (SM 802238)
145 Castell Penpleidiau (SM 763240)
146 Porth y rhaw (SM 786241)
149 Clegyr Boia (SM 737250)
150 St David's head (SM 722279)

Roman sites

16 Carmarthen town (SN 415204)
38 Cwmbrwyn (SN 254122)
41 Trelissey (SN 174077)
84 Castell Flemish (SN 007267)
84 Wolf's Castle 'villa' (SM 950264)

Dark Age sites and monuments

17 Carmarthen museum stones (SN 440209)
19 Llangunnor (SN 430203)
21 Llanfihangel Croesfeini (SN 396238)
24 Cenarth (SN 670415)
25 Cilgerran (SN 191431)
26 Bridell (SN 176421)
28 St Dogmael's (SN 163458)
29 Llanboidy (SN 216233)
32 Llangan (SN 177187)
34 Laugharne (SN 302114)
36 Llandawke (SN 283112)
37 Parc y gerrig sanctaidd (SN 269106)
39 Eglwys Cymyn (SN 231107)
52 Llawhaden (SN 075175)
57 Clydai (SN 251355)
59 Bayvil gaer (SN 113417)
61 Nevern (SN 083400)
70 Llanllawer (SM 987360)
71 Llanychaer (SM 987354)
72 Llanychlwydog (SN 012344)
73 Pontfaen (SN 022340)
80 Llandeilo (SN 099269)
86 Spittal (SM 975229)
93 Penally (SS 117992)
94 Caldey island (SS 141963)
99 Carew (SN 046037)
108 Castlemartin (SR 910988)
113 Stackpole Elidyr (SR 988973)
124 St Ishmael's (SM 830067)
125 St Bride's (SM 803108)
127 (?) Gateholm (SM 770071)
128 Deer Point (SM 760090)
136 Llanwnda (SM 932396)
139 St Nicholas (SM 900356)
140 Mathry (SM 879320)
140 Mesur y dorth (SM 837306)
143 Brawdy (SM 858240)
144 Solfa (SM 801243)
147 St David's (SM 751253)
148 St Non's (SM 751243)

Medieval churches

1 Pembrey (SN 429011)
2 Kidwelly (SN 408067)
5 St Ishmael's (SN 363084)
7 Llangyndeyrn (SN 456140)

13 Llansteffan (SN350107)
16 Carmarthen (SN 415203)
19 Llangunnor (SN 430203)
27 Cardigan (SN 180460)
33 St Clears (SN 282157)
34 Laugharne (SN 302114)
36 Llandawke (SN 283112)
39 Eglwys Cymmyn (SN 231107)
41 Marros (SN 207089)
42 Amroth (SN 163077)
43 Ludchurch (SN 140109)
45 Begelly (SN 118072)
47 Minwear (SN 039129)
52 Llawhaden (SN 075175)
55 Wiston (SN 023179)
57 Clydai (SN 251355)
61 Nevern (SN 083400)
65 Newport (SN 058389)
81 New Moat (SN 062253)
86 Spittal (SM 975229)
88 Tenby (SN 134004)
90 Gumfreston (SN 109011)
91 St Florence (SN 082011)
93 Penally (SS 117992)
94 Caldey (SS 143966)
96 Manorbier (SS 065976)
97 Hodgeston (SS 030993)
99 Carew (SN 045027)
100 Upton (SN 020046)
101 Monkton (SM 979014)
101 Pembroke St Mary's (SM 983015)
103 Pwllchrochan (SM 920026)
104 Rhoscrowther (SM 903022)
106 Angle chapel (SM 865028)
108 Catlemartin (SR 910988)
109 Flimston chapel (SR 924956)
111 Bosherston (SR 965948)
113 Stackpole Elidyr (SR 988973)
114 St Petrox (SR 971976)
115 Haverfordwest St Mary's (SM 951156)
115 Haverfordwest St Martin's (SM 951157)
118 Johnston (SM 933103)
119 Rosemarket (SM 952082)
120 Llangwm (SM 990093)
124 St Ishmael's (SM 830067)
125 St Bride's (SM 803108)
130 Rudbaxton (SM 960204)
131 Camrose (SM 927200)
132 Nolton (SM 867181)
143 Brawdy (SM 858240)
147 St David's cathedral (SM 751253)

Monastic sites

2 Kidwelly priory (SN 408067)
16 Carmarthen priory & friary (sites only)

27 Cardigan priory (SN 180460)
28 St Dogmael's abbey (SN 163458)
31 Whitland abbey (SN 208182)
33 St Clears priory (SN 282157)
94 Caldey priory (SN 141963)
101 Monkton priory (SM 979014)
115 Haverfordwest priory (SM 956152)
121 Pill priory (SM 903073)

Ruined churches & chapels

7 Capel Dyddgen (SN 465126)
14 Llanybri (SN 336125)
15 Llandeilo Abercywin (SN 309130)
15 Llanfihangel Abercywin (SN 302133)
46 Cresswell (SN 049070)
52 Llawhaden hospital (SN 066172)
53 Slebech (SN 022138)
56 Boulston (SM 979122)
80 Llandeilo (SN 099269)
110 St Govan's (SR 967929)
129 St Leonard's (SM 984188)
144 Solfa (SM 812240)
148 St Non's (SM 751243)
149 St Justinian's (SM 724252)
150 St Patrick's (SM 733272)

Holy wells

13 St Anthony's well (SN 346098)
32 Canna's well (SN 178188)
48 St Margaret's (SN 111116)
65 St Curig's (SN 058387)
70 Llanllawer (SM 987360)
80 Ffynnon Deilo (SN 099269)
82 Bernard's well (SN 954280)
90 Gumfreston wells (SN 109011)
110 St Govan's (SR 967929)
116 Higgon's well (SM 961150)
129 St Leonard's (SM 984188)
148 St Non's (SM 751243)

Houses

1 Pembrey Court (SN 428015)
4 Penallt (SN 387070)
8 Green Castle (SN 396166)
15 Llandeilo Abercywin (SN 309130)
16 Angel Vaults (SN 413200)
34 Island House (SN 302107)
46 Cresswell castle (SN 049070)
47 Sister's House (SN 033136)
48 Templeton (SN 113116)
49 Plas Farm (SN 108145)
56 Boulston old hall (SM 980123)
71 Garn, Llanychar (SM 994348)

88 Tenby houses (SN 135004)
89 Scotsborough House (SN 117010)
90 Priest's house (SN 109011)
91 West Tarr (SN 089008)
91 Carswell (SN 098010)
91 St Florence houses (SN 082011)
93 'St Deniol's chapel' (SS 117992)
94 St Margaret's island (SS 120972)
95 Lydstep (SS 086983)
98 Lamphey Bishop's Palace (SN 019008)
98 Lamphey round chimney (SN 016006)
99 Carew round chimney (SN 047037)
99 Carew rectory (SN 044027)
101 Monkton old hall (SM 980014)
101 Priory Farm (SM 978014)
101 Pembroke town houses (SM 982014)
104 Eastington (SM 901024)
106 Angle tower house (SM 866030)
106 Angle 'nunnery' (SM 865028)
108 Castlemartin 'rectory' (SR 911988)
109 Flimston (SR 924956)
111 Bosherston cottages (SR 965948)
115 Haverfordwest houses (SM 953157)
117 Haroldston (SM 957144)
119 Cross Farm (SM 952082)
120 Great Nash (SM 976100)
124 St Bride's 'abbey' (SM 804107)
132 Nolton (SM 867181)
147 St David's Palace (SM 750253)
149 Rhosson-uchaf farm (SM 727253)

Earthwork castles

15 Llanfihangel Abercywin (SN 297136)
21 Llanfihangel Croesfeini (SN 396238)
24 Cenarth (SN 269414)
29 Llanboidy (SN 219231)
33 St Clears (SN 281154)
42 Amroth (SN 163077)
48 Sentance Castle (SN 110116)
81 New Moat (SN 063253)
82 Henry's Moat (SN 044275)
83 Castlebythe (SN 021290)
122 Walwyn's Castle (SM 073030)
124 St Ishmael's (SM 835073)
129 Rudbaxton (SM 961205)
131 Camrose (SM 927198)
134 Wolf's Castle (SM 957965)
147 St David's (SM 744252)

Stone castles

2 Kidwelly (SN 409070)
13 Llansteffan (SN 351101)
16 Carmarthen (SN 413200)
23 Newcastle Emlyn (SN 311407)

25 Cilgerran (SN 195431)
27 Cardigan (SN 178459)
34 Laugharne (SN 303107)
35 Roche (SN 294102)
49 Narberth (SN 109143)
52 Llawhaden (SN 073174)
54 Picton (SN 011134)
55 Wiston (SN 023182)
61 Nevern (SN 082401)
65 Newport (SN 057388)
88 Tenby (SN 138005)
96 Manorbier (SS 064978)
99 Carew (SN 045037)
100 Upton (SN 020047)
101 Pembroke (SM 982016)
107 Angle blockhouse (SM 842027)
115 Haverfordwest (SM 953157)
133 Roch castle (SM 880212)

Miscellaneous sites

3 Pont Spwdwr bridge (SN 434058)
5 Hawton lost village (SN 37?07?)
17 Abergwili Museum (SN 440209)
22 Clawdd Mawr dyke (SN 377330)
76 Carn Meini bluestone quarry
88 Tenby castle museum (SN 138005)
96 Manorbier dovecote & mill (SS 063977)
97 Hodgeston moated site (SS 028994)
106 Angle dovecote (SM 866030)
115 Haverfordwest museum (SM 953157)
119 Rosemarket dovecote (SM 953082)
120 Great Nash dovecote (SM 976100)

Legends and curiosities

5 Hawton lost village
16 Carmarthen church
24 Cenarth beavers
32 Llangan church
37 Parc y gerrig sanctaidd
54 Picton castle
56 Boulston basilisk
61 Nevern cross
63 Bedd yr afanc
74 Cerrig Meibion Arthur
76 Stonehenge bluestones
86 Spittal treasure
92 Hoyle's Mouth cave
110 St Govan's chapel
113 Stackpole
114 St Petrox
122 Walwyn's Castle
129 Rudbaxton Rath
133 Roch Castle
137 Carn Gilfach
140 Mathry church
150 Rocking stone

Bibliography & further reading list

For those readers needing more information on west Wales there is a large number of books currently available, mainly relating to the old county of Pembrokeshire, Few, however, deal exclusively with ancient monuments.

One of the latest (and certainly the most entertaining) is Roger Worsley's 'The Pembrokeshire Explorer' (1988), but there are many others, and the Coast Park Authorities have produced several little guides, including one on castles. For the bibliophile there are a number of early works to hunt up; Gerald of Wales' rambling account of his 'Journey through Wales' in 1188 (available in modern translations), George Owen's 'History of Pembrokeshire' (1603), and Williams Camden's 'Britannia' (the 1722 edition revised by Edward Llwyd).

Closer to our own times there is Richard Fenton's 'Tours in Wales' & 'A Historical tour through Pembrokeshire' (1811), and Edward Laws' 'The History of the Little England Beyond Wales' (1888). The main reference source for archaeological material is the Carmarthenshire and Pembrokeshire inventories, published in 1917 and 1925 by the Royal Commission on Ancient & Historic Monuments. Articles on sites in west Wales can also be gleaned from the pages of yearly journals such as 'Archaeology in Wales', 'The Carmarthenshire Antiquary' and 'Archaeologia Cambrensis'. The following list of books is split-up into categories for those interested in a particular historic period.

Stone & Bronze Age:

The Upper Paleolithic of Britain (1977) J. Cambell
Prehistoric Man in Wales and the west (1972) F. Lynch & C. Burgess
The Prehistory of Wales (1951) W. F. Grimes
The Prehistoric Chamber Tombs of England & Wales (1950) G. Daniel

Iron Age:

Hillforts of Britain (1975) A. H. A. Hogg
Fighting and Farming in Iron Age West Wales (1985) G. Williams

Roman:

Roman West Wales (1982) H. James

Dark Ages:

Wales in the Early Middle Ages (1982) W. Davies
The Early Christian Monuments of Wales (1950) V. E. Nash-Williams

Middle Ages:

Castles of Dyfed (1987) P. R. Davis
Castles (1982) AA & Wales Tourist Board
Cathedral, Abbeys & Priories (1986) H. Thorold
Welsh Parish Churches (1984) R. W. Soden
Houses of the Welsh Countryside (1975) P. Smith
Medieval Religious Houses (1971) D. Knowles & R. Hadcock
Holy Wells of Wales (1954) F. Jones